Leicester Mercury

The Illustrated History of

LEICESTER'S SUBURBS

CHRISTINE JORDAN

Christine Jordan

First published in Great Britain in 2003 by
The Breedon Books Publishing Company Limited
Breedon House, 3 The Parker Centre,
Derby, DE21 4SZ.

ISBN 1 85983 348 9

Printed and bound by Butler & Tanner,
Frome, Somerset, England.

Cover printing by Lawrence-Allen Colour Printers,
Weston-super-Mare, Somerset, England.

Contents

Introduction

This book traces the history of the suburbs within the boundary of the city of Leicester, and although it provides no more than an overview of each one, it is hoped that the most important and unusual features have not been excluded. For people who have lived in a particular suburb for many years and know it far more intimately than I could ever hope to do, I am sure to have omitted some well-loved landmark or a particularly eccentric resident, for which I can only offer my apologies! I have tried to consider each suburb from its inception or expansion, where a village had previously existed for several hundred years. This book is merely a taster for those who might wish to do further research, as several thousand words could be written on each suburb.

The book considers the architectural and social history of each area, with greater emphasis on the latter half of the 19th century and the first half of the 20th. Documentary evidence, both written and illustrative, becomes far more abundant over this period. During the Victorian era (1837–1901) more records began to be kept, such as the census, which took place each decade from 1841. Building plans began to be deposited with local councils, although not all had the foresight (as in Leicester) to preserve them until this became compulsory much later in the 20th century. Ordnance Survey maps were also produced from the 19th century and these too are invaluable in tracing the development of different areas. In the 1900s many parts of Leicester were still rural but by the 1920s were largely built up. The OS maps provide a fascinating insight into what was there before. The development of photography grew apace from the 1850s, providing previously unimaginable images of landscapes, buildings and people, thus making an immense contribution to recorded history. The photographs in the book are all from the extensive archives of the Leicester, Leicestershire and Rutland Record Office and the *Leicester Mercury*. The pictures themselves tell the story of the development of suburban Leicester, from Queen Victoria to Queen Elizabeth II.

The Roman town of Leicester, known as Ratae Corieltauvorum, had its own suburban developments and evidence was discovered in the 17th century of highly decorative tessellated pavements in the suburb of Westcotes. The Romans were followed by the Saxons, Danes and Normans. Richard Gill speculates in his excellent *Book of Leicester*, that the city's best known and probably favourite expression 'mi duck' is a derivative of the Danish word for doll. Suburbanites may feel themselves above such idiomatic expressions!

Very early history is always a problem and even entries in the Domesday Book are not always as detailed as they could be – although they mention 'meadows', no other uncultivated land is taken into account. Paul M. Dare, writing in the 1920s, mentions that the measurements of land are very confusing. He is quite right! Hides, ploughs and caracutes are not only puzzling but also inaccurate, as they do not translate well into a modern equivalent. To make matters even more confusing, Leicestershire had some measurements of its own. However, much information from the Domesday Survey, compiled in 1086, is invaluable in building up some kind of picture of life in the area over 900 years ago.

The spelling of names of people and villages is also a problem – the variations are endless. Hugh de Grentemesnil, who makes a number of appearances in this book, could have as many twists on his name! The approach I have taken is to use the spelling that appears most frequently. The names of the suburbs themselves can have a variety of different forms and spellings, which have evolved over the centuries. The meanings of these names are also open to interpretation, and the name Belgrave, for example, appears to have undergone three or four changes of meaning.

Leicester and Leicestershire are of course recorded in the Domesday Book. Some villages, thriving concerns in the 11th century, disappeared within a few hundred years, only to be revived as a suburb in later years. One such lost village was Bromkinsthorpe, also known as Bruntingthorpe and not to be confused with the village of the same name that still exists. Bromkinsthorpe re-emerged in the 18th century as Westcotes.

Much of Leicester's wealth in the 19th century was founded on the boot, shoe and hosiery industries. There were also many subsidiaries to these industries, companies like the British United Shoe Machinery Company, a name which speaks for itself, with its huge factory on Belgrave Road. There were companies such as Faire Brothers, who were rather like haberdashers to the boot and shoe industry. There were endless elastic web manufacturers. Hosiery manufacturers became household names: Corahs's, Pex, Chilprufe, Wolsley and many others. Other well-known products made in Leicester were Remington and Imperial Typewriters, Kendall's Umbrellas and Goddard's Silver Polish. The owners and managers of many of the town's successful businesses lived in the most fashionable suburban areas. The town had a buoyant economy, particularly after the 1870s, and continued to prosper until the outbreak of World War One in 1914. The successful economy meant that more and more factories were required to maintain the high rate of production. The war did not deter the many small manufacturers and the city continued to prosper throughout the 1920s and 1930s. Such was its wealth that in 1936 the Bureau of Statistics of the League of Nations declared Leicester the second richest city in Europe. For a city that had only become a city in 1919, then a cathedral city in 1927 when the parish church of St Martin was consecrated, this was a rather elevated position.

The prosperous foundations of Leicester were built by its many nonconformist manufacturers, many of whom were councillors and Lord Mayors of the borough or city. Many, like John and William Biggs, who were the town's major hosiery manufacturers in the mid-19th century, were Unitarians. The brothers were both mayor of Leicester three times.

While increased industrialisation brought prosperity to the town, it was also one of the main reasons for the serious overcrowding and insanitary conditions that were a fact of life in many towns and cities in the 19th century. It was the serious concerns about these conditions that prompted the town to reach out into the suburbs. As the town grew, so did its population: in 1861 it was 68,000, but by 1871 it had risen dramatically to 95,000 and in 1901 the population had more than doubled in 30 years to 219,000. From the 1860s a considerable amount of building took place and thousands of houses were built in streets off the Belgrave and Melton Roads, forming the suburb of Belgrave, which had previously been a village. Most of those houses still exist today. Highfields, Newfoundpool, the West End and Westcotes all began to be built up in the closing decades of the 19th century. By the start of the 20th century some of the areas were virtually complete. As the new suburban areas began to develop they acquired their own specialist shops and by the early 20th century nearly all would have a branch of the Leicester Co-operative Society. Many also had a branch of Worthington's Cash Stores Limited, as well as an outlet of another local chain of grocers, Goodall's. Often families had a particular preference for one or the other. Wealthier suburbanites could shop at Simpkin and James on Horsefair Street and have the groceries delivered. This was a service many shops provided, whether by a boy on a bicycle or a smart liveried van. Some specialist suburban shops continued to offer this service until the 1990s.

The expanding town also needed an efficient transport system, since the population and workplaces were no longer confined to the central districts. The first tramlines to take the new horse-drawn trams were built in 1873. They ran from the Clock Tower, with the first three routes running 1½ miles along the London Road; 1¾ miles along the Belgrave Road and just over a mile along the Humberstone Road. The fare was 2d for two miles or less and 1d per mile for more than a two-mile journey. Electric trams were introduced in 1904 and motorbuses were added to supplement these in 1925. The tram service in Leicester finally ceased operating in 1949.

In 1914 World War One brought a halt to many building projects. A subsequent shortage of labour and materials meant that little building work was carried out until the early 1920s. Many architects had to take alternative employment during the war years, because of the lack of available work. After hostilities ended in 1918, the report of a parliamentary committee, which had held an inquiry into housing conditions in England, Wales and Scotland, concluded that one million houses were needed within five years to house the working population. The following year the Housing and Town Planning Act 1919 gave many local authorities the power to compulsorily purchase large estates on the fringes of towns and cities. In some instances the wealthy owners were absentee landlords and thus relatively happy to sell off a part or all of their Leicester estates. They no longer had to worry about poor harvests or finding agricultural workers for the tenant farms. The boot, shoe and hosiery industries had become more attractive areas of employment for those living only two or three miles from the city centre. The hours were shorter, the pay was better and you could cycle to work, or walk to the nearest stop on the ever-expanding tram network. For some of the landed gentry, the 'servant problem' after World War One also had to be addressed. Working in industry was more attractive than being 'in service'. The servant shortage became acute and trying to maintain a large house, with gardens and an estate, became impossible. It was therefore with reluctance tempered with relief that many wealthy landowners disposed of their property to avoid staff problems and crippling taxation.

Some landowners, however, were desperately unhappy about giving up old houses that had been in the same family for generations, not to mention their pleasant lifestyle, carried on within a large and beautiful estate. In Leicester one such was Major Richard Winstanley, who lived with his family at Braunstone Hall. His ancestors had lived there for around 300 years and in 1911, only a few years before the outbreak of war, he had had the hall modernised and extended. He also had a young family, who were very happy in their surroundings. Parliament and local government, however, needed the land for building and Major Winstanley was forced to sell in 1925. The land was needed for local authority housing, but the government realised that there was also the 'private sector' to consider.

Not all builders wanted to work for the local authority and Leicester had a number of good, reliable, small building firms, some of whom were used consistently over the years by the city's major architects. In the 19th century it was much more common to rent a house, and it was usually only the very wealthy who owned property. After World War One, it became easier to obtain a mortgage and more people wanted to own their own home. Two common expressions of the time were 'Homes Fit For Heroes', for those returning from World War One, and 'A Home of Our Own', a heartfelt sentiment that meant not sharing a house with anyone, whether it be the in-laws or a private landlord from whom you rented a couple of rooms. These slogans often appeared on posters and in advertising. The Government was desperate to increase the housing stock as much as possible and in the 1920s passed the Building Subsidy Act, which meant that the government met 20 percent of the cost of building in the private sector. There were of course restrictions: builders could only build three or four-bedroomed houses on a certain amount of land. Many houses were built, as they had been in the 19th century, on a speculative basis, and the builder could then either lease or sell them as he chose. Other houses were specially commissioned and, despite the servant shortage, some were still built to accommodate staff. In the 1920s some four-bedroomed suburban houses were built with two of the bedrooms being for maids. In the 1900s in Leicester, a similarly sized house would often have one small bedroom for two servants.

The overcrowding that the new building was meant to improve was not a result of World War One but had existed for centuries and had become acute since the onset of industrialisation in the 19th century, which had caused the flood of people into towns and cities to work in the factories. It was this that really brought about the crowded and insanitary conditions in cities such as Leicester. The Edwardian period (1901–1910) saw many different styles of housing and it was really the final decade of the terraced house. This was the period when the garden city and suburb really began to emerge as better housing options. Space, light, fresh air and a generally more healthy atmosphere had previously only been available to the few, and had not been seriously considered until the second half of the 19th century. For those who could afford it in Leicester, this was the period when people began to gradually move away from fashionable 18th-century addresses in the town, swapping a three-storey Georgian terrace in Mill Lane or Princess Road for a large two-storey house with a garden near the racecourse on the London Road, or in Westcotes.

The suburbs of Leicester were not exclusively wealthy areas. Knighton and Stoneygate were the most affluent and firmly established by the beginning of the 20th century, but there was still room for the artisans. Aylestone Park, Clarendon Park and Westcotes had large numbers of terraced houses in varying degrees of size and style, together with much grander properties in their own grounds. Within a mile or so of these areas there were a number of shoe and hosiery factories and many other small business. In North Evington, eminent architect Arthur Wakerley designed most of the Crown Hills area over a 40-year period. This was an area predominantly for the factory worker and the artisan and unlike some suburban areas, the factories were an integral part of the layout, enabling workers to walk to work.

By the early 20th century many of the better-off middle classes had moved to the suburbs. They could travel the two or three miles into the town using their own horse-drawn transport or by taking a tram. By the end of the first decade of the new century the motor car was beginning to become the favoured mode of transport for the wealthier middle classes. Within two or three years of purchasing a new house in Western Park or Stoneygate, the addition of a 'motor house' was deemed essential. These would sometimes be of two storeys, so that the chauffeur could be housed as well. Few people could drive at the time, and saw no need to if someone could do it for them. As car ownership increased in the years after World War One, some innovative architects began to design houses with integral garages.

There were many different styles of housing in the late 19th and early 20th century, with a number being built in the Arts and Crafts style. These would often be built of local materials, red brick with a Swithland slate roof, even though by this time local slate was somewhat scarce, making it a rather exclusive commodity, the quarry having closed in the late 19th century. There was a brickworks in the city as late as the 1960s. Other features would include roughcast rendering, stained and leaded windows, gables and steeply pitched roofs. Many had good sized gardens and some had half an acre or more of land. In the very select areas of Knighton and Stoneygate they might have several acres.

Suburban houses built after World War One continued in a similar vein, whether they were privately owned or built by the borough. Consideration was given to space, with gardens for recreation and the cultivation of fruit and vegetables. The suburban gardens of Leicester became miniature versions of those that were part of the grand estates, on whose land many were built. From the 1920s the semi-detached house became the most popular variety of housing for the private sector. A number of council houses were also built in pairs, as well as in blocks of four that were often designed to resemble a pair.

The 1930s saw further suburban expansion, with the addition of new roads and more housing, often the ubiquitous 'semi' but in Leicester usually interspersed with detached houses. This type of housing gave rise to derogatory comments from many writers. From the 1930s to the 1950s there were many articles and cartoons about life in suburbia. Past writers have often been of the opinion that the suburbs are dull and soulless, but they cannot possibly be referring to Leicester when they say this! The rich variety of the semi-detached house in Leicester is quite remarkable. Many are built of the local red brick, but rarely without a design in the brickwork. A walk along Leicester's suburban roads reveals a staggering amount of variation. Doors, some still with brass name plates; windows, with coloured and leaded glass; different gables and porches; not to mention gates and gardens; all refuting any idea that the suburbs are all bland and boring.

After World War Two the city continued to flourish and expand, although not all its housing schemes were a success, particularly where these contained tower blocks. Many estates, however, which consisted mostly of houses, worked very well, such as New Parks, and Eyres Monsell, where there are many lush green spaces. Perhaps surprisingly, it seems to be the 1960s and 1970s that brought the greatest change to the suburban landscape. At this time the last few farms were swallowed up to come within the city boundary, and allotments and other green spaces were used for building and new roads. The private sector continues to build in the suburbs when land becomes available. Former dairies, factories, swimming pools and shops have reached the end of their useful life and have been demolished and replaced by housing. Many important buildings have been saved from destruction and 'modernisation' by a more enlightened attitude and the realisation that we need to preserve our heritage. The suburban house is part of that heritage and Leicester has some of the finest examples. There are a number of listed buildings and conservation areas in suburban Leicester. Developers now realise the importance of blending in the new with the old and some very pleasing and imaginative schemes have emerged since the 1980s.

The suburbs are not, as they are often portrayed, rows of identical 1930s semi-detached houses stretching along the arterial routes and major ring roads with more packed in behind them. A visitor to Leicester negotiating ring roads, bus lanes and one-way systems might not have time to notice how diverse areas are, but there is no question that each part is different. Parks, gardens, allotments, trees, roundabouts, plant containers and hanging baskets make Leicester a very green city. Churches, from the mediaeval to the modern, some by renowned architects of the Victorian period, like Sir George Gilbert Scott, who designed St Pancras Station, are interesting landmarks. In the 1950s architects such as Basil Spence, who designed Coventry Cathedral, produced designs for suburban churches in Leicester. Religious buildings of all denominations add to the individual identity of an area, and Leicester's multi-cultural population has added a great deal in the past 30 years. Schools, colleges, libraries, municipal buildings, sculpture, bridges and commercial buildings, from the middle of the 19th century to the present day, all bring something to the city. Each suburban area has its own history: whether it stretches back as far as the Romans, or has less than a century of development, it is nevertheless a history. Even though there may not have been a village or large country house with extensive grounds on a site, there was usually some kind of cultivated or grazing land and an absentee landlord. Western Park and Eyres Monsell are both examples of this.

A suburb, be it a municipal estate or a private development, is rarely just an extension of the city; it is a separate community, often with a village atmosphere. This sense of community is most apparent in suburban Leicester. Many people moved out to the suburbs as children and have often stayed in the same areas, as have their children and grandchildren. People move house of course, but in many areas of Leicester, despite having scoured the city and county for a property, people are just as likely to move round the corner! The suburbanites who have a particular affinity with their area find it difficult to leave and even if they do, they often return, finding the area they like the most is their own.

-o0o-

Where then to begin with charting the history of the suburbs? A suburb that exists now may not have existed at all in 1891 when boundary changes took place, or it may have been outside the city boundary and, therefore, a village in its own right. There may well have been objections to being swallowed up into the ever-expanding town of Leicester and losing the particular individuality that gives a village its identity. Boundary changes in the 19th century saw a great expansion of Leicester in 1835. In 1891 it was even greater and took in the villages of Belgrave, Knighton, Aylestone, North Evington and West Humberstone.

Boundary changes apart, anomalies also occur when areas have been thought of as suburban over many decades. In some parts of Leicester the separation of city and county is scarcely discernable. Examples of this are New Parks and Glenfield, the two halves of Braunstone and West Knighton and Wigston. The type of housing or the rate of expansion, together with the shrinking of the old village centre, are the main factors in the blurring of identity between village and suburb.

Other problems in writing a history of this nature are the definitions of each area where they merge together. Some people have very clear ideas about the roads that form the boundaries of these areas, but a parish border might give a different line. Some maps use older names: the Western Park area is usually referred to as such but on some maps appears as the Dane Hills; parts of Westcotes are deemed to be the West End but this name is usually associated with most of the Narborough Road area. Some areas developed in the 1970s and 1980s have been omitted because there is little in terms of historical development to include. There were some buildings that I particularly wanted to include where no photographs existed. Some have been demolished or so radically altered in their present guise as to be virtually unrecognisable.

Some areas are very small and not well documented and have had to be excluded. Some local authority housing estates have proved problematic in terms of historical information and therefore have a mainly photographic history. The Leicester City Council Minutes held some delightful snippets of information applying to the relatively new phenomenon of the council house. The Housing Committee Minutes for 1926 noted that there were no objections to tenants having wireless sets in their new council houses on the various municipal estates that were rapidly spreading through the outer suburbs of Leicester.

Many publications were consulted in the process of writing this book, together with copies of the *Leicester Mercury* and its forerunners and numerous trade directories. *The Victoria County Histories* are an invaluable source of detailed information; the breadth of information they contain is exceptional. The two volumes of *Leicester Past and Present* by Jack Simmons are also excellent sources on the history of Leicester. Malcolm Elliott in *Victorian Leicester* provides a very interesting and detailed history of the town in the 19th century.

The Book of Leicester by Richard Gill, as previously mentioned, provides a closer look at the city's buildings. David Nash and David Reeder, the editors of *Leicester in the Twentieth Century*, present an informed view of the city over the past hundred years.

ACKNOWLEDGEMENTS

I am indebted to a great many people in compiling this book, indeed without whose help and encouragement I would not have embarked on the project at all! My thanks are due to the following: Alex and Chris Jordan for their additional research and having to live in an even more chaotic household than usual, as I wrote and researched. Rowan Roenisch and Malcolm Elliott, not only for their expertise on Leicester and its buildings, but also for kindly reading through the manuscript. Janet Myles and Peter Walton for looking at the work in its early stages, together with my colleagues om HAMC 1014, Emily Baines, Ruth Brompton and Pam Inder. Horace Gamble, Gordon Harle, Steve Hill and David Waldram for information on transport. All the members of the Leicester Victorian Society Buildings Sub-Committee, particularly Gwyn Jones, Jon Goodall and Mike Taylor. Steve and Georgianne Green, Clare and Geoff Pollard, Liz Watson and Julie Beachall. I would particularly like to thank Adam Goodwin for his help and good humour on all occasions I plundered the archives of the Leicester, Leicestershire and Rutland Record Office and Leicester Archaeological and Historical Society Librarian. All the Record Office staff who were unfailingly helpful, despite the chaos of major building works. Steve England and his staff at the *Leicester Mercury* library, who supplied the remainder of the photographs and other archive material, cheerfully accommodated my frequent visits in pursuit of these. My apologies to anyone who has been unintentionally omitted. Every effort has been made to comply with copyright regulations with regard to all the illustrations; the photograph of Knighton Fields House is my own.

AYLESTONE

Pleasant terraced housing with decorative brickwork on Wigston Lane, c.1900.

Aylestone or Ailstone (there are also other variations), is approximately 2½ miles from the city centre and is divided into two areas, the old village of Aylestone and Aylestone Park. Aylestone Park was the name given to the 19th-century development between the old village of Aylestone and Leicester. It was precisely this development that linked village and town to form the suburban district of Aylestone. This became part of the borough of Leicester in 1891 as a result of the Leicester Extension Act of the same year. The old village of Aylestone is listed in the Domesday Book of 1086 as being held by the Count of Meulan, who had the equivalent of 120 acres of land. The Domesday survey also recorded that there were four mills, valued at 48 shillings, and one female slave! The very early mills did not survive but a corn mill was recorded much later in 1846. So by the 11th century the village was already quite large.

Thomas Biggs's Boathouse, Middleton Street, where boats, punts and canoes were for hire or a game of bowls or tennis could be played. The board also declares: 'Teas and Refreshments Provided'. The boathouse operated from about 1911 until the outbreak of World War Two.

Aylestone Meadows from the railway, a picturesque scene, with a lady cyclist descending the bridge. Middleton Street and the boathouse are also visible.

There is evidence that the parish church of St Andrew was built in the 13th century but various sources suggest that it may well be somewhat earlier, possibly of Saxon origin, although with the exception of a triangular headed window in the north wall of the tower, now only visible from the inside, there is little evidence to substantiate this. A further early structure in Aylestone is the old packhorse bridge at the end of Marsden Lane, which is likely to be 15th-century and is believed to be one of the oldest bridges in Leicestershire. This was built to accommodate the traffic that arose from the increase in the coal trade between Leicester and Swannington.

The ownership of land in Aylestone passed through a variety of people until the middle of the 15th century when it came into the possession of the Manners family. On the death of Sir George Vernon in 1565 his youngest daughter Dorothy and her husband Sir John Manners inherited the manor together with Haddon Hall and other manors in Derbyshire. There are romantic stories that Dorothy eloped with John Manners, but this seems to be conjecture. Her father bequeathed Haddon Hall to her on his death, so it seems unlikely that she had disgraced the family. It is thought that she married in St Andrew's church, but there are no surviving records. Dorothy's attractiveness is referred to in many publications, but this may be ascribed to poetic licence. Her legend came to prominence in the early 19th century when Eliza Meteyard, who wrote under the pseudonym 'Silverpen', produced a short story with the title *Dorothy Vernon.* This was a rather embellished and saccharine version of the possible elopement. It also appears to be the first time that any suggestion of an elopement appeared in print, some 250 years after the event! The legend probably arose because Sir George felt that the Manners family were not quite good enough for his daughter, as they had only been elevated to the peerage in 1526. The name Dorothy Vernon was also used in the 20th century by a Leicestershire hosiery company, as the logo for its high quality silk stockings, available in 1932 for 3s 11d.

The Manners family, the Dukes of Rutland, continued their ownership of the manor until Charles John Cecil decided to sell the estate in 1869, the sale taking place at the Temperance Hall, Leicester, on 4 June that year. Many of the Duke's former tenants were able to buy their farms and cottages. The sale of land led not only to the growth of Aylestone, but also to the creation of the suburb of Rowley Fields. Aylestone Hall, part of which had been a girls boarding school in 1846 and eight years later was the residence of Joseph Knight, subsequently passed to land agent Nathaniel Stone, who with his family had been the tenant there for some years after this. Aylestone Hall then had a somewhat chequered history. After two other residents the hall was passed to Leicester City Council

A pony and trap with St Andrew's Church in the background.

in 1950, being owned by them for 50 years until it changed hands again.

Life in Aylestone passed by relatively uneventfully until the Civil War of 1645, when in May King Charles I and his nephew Prince Rupert decided to mount an attack on Leicester. Approaching from the direction of Leicester, using the packhorse bridge, they lodged in Aylestone, probably at the hall or the rectory. Prince Rupert positioned his main battery in the meadows by the River Soar, between the south wall of Leicester and Aylestone. Parliamentarian Leicester was briefly taken by the Royalists but on 14 June 1645 the king travelled through Leicester on his retreat from Naseby. A procession to mark the anniversary of the siege of Leicester takes place each year.

The waterways are one of Aylestone's most attractive features, and until the first half of the 20th century the most practical. The River Soar runs through Aylestone and in 1794 it was canalised. The route ran from Loughborough, through Aylestone to Blaby. By

A very early photograph of the Union Inn, Middleton Street. Joseph Toon was the landlord at the outbreak of World War One in 1914.

Kings Lock in the early 20th century. The girl in the large hat is Miss Harrison. Harrison's Seeds had their trial grounds behind the lock house. The Harrison family lived at 'Overdale', where Conaglen Road now stands. The lock keeper from 1900 to 1922 was George Swanick, whose wife and son Arthur are seen on the towpath.

1809 it had reached Market Harborough and by 1814 it was possible to travel to London via a link with the Grand Junction Canal. In the early 1900s Aylestone could still boast a water mill, which was used for grinding corn. The owner, a Mr Wilson, also owned Aylestone Lock. People wishing to walk between Aylestone Road and the towpath had to pass through the mill yard, where Mr Wilson charged them a halfpenny for the privilege! At Kings Lock, which was named after a previous lockkeeper, George King, who retired in 1874, there was and still is a tiny lock house. The house had only one door and no windows to the rear, perhaps to keep the lockkeeper's mind on his job as well as for economy. The land at the back of the house was used as trial grounds by seed-growers Harrison and Sons. John Harrison Senior lived at 'Overdale' on Marsden Lane.

Transport for many commercial purposes had been solved by the building of the canals at the end of the 18th century, but the roads did not fare so well. In the 1780s the state of the road between Leicester and Lutterworth was such a cause for concern that the inhabitants of Aylestone petitioned Parliament in the hope that the road would be repaired, as it was practically impossible for carriages to pass in winter. Despite an Act being passed, the road through the village remained in an appalling state. William Bickerstaffe, who was curate at St Andrew's in 1786, declared that he found it difficult to reach his home in Leicester during the winter. The curate also had to contend with the eccentricities of the vicar, the Reverend Thomas Manners, who also served the church of Willoughby but often disappeared without telling his curate of his whereabouts. The Reverend Bickerstaffe, clearly a man of action, attempted to set up a village school towards the end of the 18th century and approached the Duke of Rutland with his request, although only permission for a Sunday school was granted.

Formal education became available in Aylestone when the National School Society established a school in 1844. *Wrights Directory* of 1878 describes it as 'a neat Gothic building'. Lansdowne Road School was opened in 1881 to serve the rapidly expanding Aylestone Park area. When the new Granby Road Board School opened on 26 August 1889 building work was still in progress and reports refer to the ill-discipline and inattention of the pupils, who found greater amusement in watching the workmen. One of Granby Road's more famous pupils was the Leicester City and England goalkeeper Peter Shilton. He lived at the end house on Middlesex Road, which overlooked the

A picnic in Aylestone Meadows in the late 19th century.

goalpost of the football ground on the local playing field. Schoolboy years studying the game at close quarters obviously paid off.

The writer John Throsby noted on his visit to Aylestone in 1790 that the village was low lying with about 60 scattered houses. He also commented on the church: 'There is a singers loft newly built, and a neat pulpit'. Throsby also mentions 'an industrious uncle of mine, Mr William Throsby,' who made his fortune collecting manure from Leicester, much to the envy of his previously disparaging neighbours.

The Holt, Middleton Street, the former rectory for St Andrew's, designed by William Parsons in 1839. Sadly derelict by 1966 it was demolished two years later.

William Cobbet, the eminent 19th-century author and political journalist, who founded what was to become the parliamentary journal *Hansard*, visited Aylestone in 1830 and was horrified by the living conditions of the poor, particularly when compared with those of the vicar. He described their homes as 'miserable sheds' and the inhabitants as 'wretched', and notes 'the surprising contrast' between these and the 'fine house' of the parson. The Reverend Beresford, the parson at the time when Cobbett was writing, had a rather good deal going. He had actually become the rector of St Andrew's, Holborn, but had married a daughter of the vicar of Hoby, who had also taken the living of Aylestone. This enabled Beresford to continue living in the commodious rectory when he was not in London! Despite Cobbet's remarks, Nicholas Pevsner, writing in the 20th century, suggests that such

A steam train on the Great Central Railway crossing the bridge over the River Soar.

cottages are 'quite comfy' and 'surprisingly durable', with walls that were two feet thick and with thatched roofs. Those in Aylestone and Leicestershire generally were unusual, being of only one storey. At the time of Cobbet's visit, Aylestone could boast four public houses and a number of tradespeople.

Although conditions had improved later in the 19th century, gathering firewood was still an essential requirement of the poor. The *Leicester Advertiser* of 30 March 1895 records that two general labourers went out to gather sticks in the Dovecotes Close on Sunday 26 March 1895, despite a ferocious storm. An oak tree suddenly uprooted by the fierceness of the storm fell upon them, killing them both. At the inquest the jurors gave their fees to the two widows, a total of two sovereigns. It was a noble gesture but only a very temporary respite for the two women and their families. Aylestone seemed to have more than its fair share of tragic events. The *Supplement to the Leicester Mercury and Leicester Chronicle,* 30 January 1897, carried the dramatic headline 'The Shocking Ice Fatality in Leicester' and went on to say that three boys, two 14-year-olds and one only 10 years of age, had drowned in the vicinity of Old Aylestone.

The population grew slowly over the centuries, dropping slightly in 1871 to 450, possibly as a result of the sale of the Rutland estate, when some of the workers may have left to seek employment elsewhere. A decade later the 1881 census records the population as being 2,546, a vast increase. Many of these people were housed in Aylestone Park, the northerly area of the parish, which had developed rapidly from the 1870s. A further 45 acres of land had been auctioned in 1870. The land could be purchased relatively cheaply and people were of the opinion that not only would the suburb of Aylestone Park develop rapidly, but also that land would increase greatly in value. The fact was that despite a number of wealthy manufacturers building their houses on the main Aylestone Road, the area did not develop that speedily and even by the 1920s the expectations of a rise in land value had not been fulfilled. R.G. Waddington wrote in *The Illustrated Leicester Chronicle* of 2 May 1931 that '... for 30 or 40 years after their purchase, they found their bit of earth worth no more than they gave for it.' He also noted that there was still a substantial amount of land for sale in 1931. He mused on the fact that the '... dreary stretch of road that separates the suburb from the town...' may have been the reason for such slow development. One of the first roads to be laid out in the new suburb was Richmond Road. The eminent author and scientist C.P. Snow was born at No.40 in 1905. Ironically the road is still largely the same, with the exception of Albert Villas, Nos 40 and 42, which were demolished. Lord Snow (he was created a life peer in 1964) was educated at Alderman Newton's Grammar School and Cambridge.

In the same area Grace Road Cricket Ground was opened in 1878, on 16 acres of land purchased by the Leicestershire Cricket Ground Company. Twelve acres were devoted to running and cycling. The first cricket season opened with Leicestershire playing against Australia, the first time this had happened at county level, although it was the visiting

Aylestone Mill and lock, owned in the early 1900s by Mr Wilson.

team that won. Leicestershire were to beat them a decade later in 1888. Arthur Pougher (1865–1926) was one of Leicestershire's most successful players in the late 19th century, being in the team that beat the Australians at Lords in 1896. After his retirement he ran the Old Cricket Ground Hotel in Aylestone Park. 1878 also saw the completion of the Leicester to Aylestone tram route. The trams were horse drawn until 5 September 1904, when the new electric tram service came into operation.

Aylestone Hall, associated with Dorothy Vernon and owned for many years by the dukes of Rutland, photographed in October 1924.

The ever-expanding town encroached on the nearby villages and by the time of the 1891 census Aylestone had unquestionably become a suburb of Leicester. This in turn led to the division of the ecclesiastical parish and the need for a further Church of England. St James's, Aylestone Park, was built in the same year. The church was designed by Leicester architects R.J. and J. Goodacre and opened in 1891. The following year Aylestone was incorporated into the borough of Leicester. The population of the new suburb continued to increase rapidly and in 1901 was 7,426, a figure which doubled in the inter-war period of 1921–1931. The borough boundary was extended again in 1935, taking in part of the old civil parish, previously in Lubbesthorpe. This included the Southfields housing estate, for which the church of St Christopher was built in 1929.

The interesting little library on Richmond Road opened in 1896, its quirky design and tiny façade belying a delightful interior with the original fireplace still intact, if not in use. Long may it remain. Next door, on the corner with Lansdowne Road, was the Police and Fire Station. A working men's club had been formed towards the end of the 19th century, moving in 1903 to a sizeable new building on Saffron Lane. Aylestone Baths, built at a cost of £6,000, opened in 1910, providing leisure activities for both sexes and being one of the first baths to daringly introduce mixed bathing in 1912. An added dimension was that the swimming pool could be covered and used as a dance floor. Other secular diversions in Aylestone were greatly enhanced by the opening of the Aylestone cinema in 1926, complete with an eight-piece orchestra to accompany the silent films. The *Leicester Mercury* of 29 July 1968, reporting on its closure, tells that Frederick Stafford had been the sole owner since its opening and had supervised its construction.

Another view of the hall in October 1924.

A shiny new van climbs the canal bridge in the summer of 1951. The bridge was demolished in 1958.

Chatting about the fish on the old packhorse bridge in 1921.

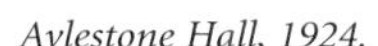

Aylestone Hall, 1924.

Another popular leisure activity in Aylestone, particularly during the summer months, was taking advantage of the facilities provided by the old boathouse. Canoes and punts were for hire, there were tennis courts and teas and innumerable other activities. Biggs's Boat House was a popular venue from around the turn of the 20th century. The *Leicester Mercury* of 11 February 1985, reporting on its impending demolition, notes: 'More than half a century earlier courting couples spent many a romantic evening strolling along the canal. They drifted along in punts and canoes with fairy lights twinkling in the dusk, or perhaps played tennis on a lazy summer afternoon.' The *Mercury* added that names were given to parts of the canal, such as 'Hiawatha's Rapids' and 'Parting Pool', the latter possibly recalling the departure of men called up for national service to fight in both World Wars.

During World War One, the recreation ground in Aylestone was turned into a large potato patch to supplement the limited supply of vegetables available in the shops. Strangely one of the more major dramas occurred in Aylestone between the wars, when in August 1931 one of a group of five vast night-bombing aeroplanes was forced to make an emergency landing only 15 yards from the railway embankment. The incident made the front page of the *Leicester Mercury* on 10 August 1931, and reported that after the pilot's successful landing: 'there were soon hundreds of children on the spot, and they surged round the pilot clamouring for his autograph.' During World War Two, a bomb fell on Cavendish Road on 21 August 1940. Six people were killed and 24 injured, seven of them seriously. The bombing was the work of a lone raider with eight high-explosive bombs, who missed his prime target, the gasworks.

Number 77, Hughendon Drive, Aylestone Park. The end of an era: the far from temporary prefabs erected after World War Two are demolished in 1972.

Aylestone's diversity is reflected in the difference between the busy commercial stretch of road from the gasworks to Middleton Street and the tranquil meadows, hidden behind houses and factories. The mediaeval ridge and furrow farming system can still be seen in local fields. The river and canal flow through the suburb, still used by narrowboats. The lockkeeper's cottage is still in use, but has recently been put up for sale, hopefully with a proviso that the new owner can also operate the locks. The different seasons produce numerous wild flowers and fruits. The passing places on the packhorse bridge allow the walker to wait for the jogger to speed past instead of the equine transport of the Middle Ages. Aylestone is a prime example of suburbia being not what it seems.

Further reading:

Braund, J. and J. Evans, *Old Aylestone*, Anderson Publications, 1983.
Dare, P.M., *Aylstone Manor and Church*, Edgar Backus, 1924.
Lee, J. *Who's Buried Where in Leicestershire*, Leicester Libraries and Information Service, 1991.

Beaumont Leys

Beaumont Leys is situated two miles north-west of Leicester; it was once part of Leicester Forest and was probably named after Robert de Beaumont who was created 1st Earl of Leicester by William the Conqueror. Although the 11th century is the earliest date that Beaumont Leys is recorded there is evidence that Castle Hill, now Castle Hill Country Park, was first occupied around 200 BC. Flints excavated from the site in 1984 suggest that they are indicative of the Late Neolithic or Early Bronze Age. There is also evidence of Roman occupation beginning in the second half of the first century AD until the fourth century. Henry VIII granted right to pasturage for cows and horses of poor inhabitants. The historian John Leland wrote in around 1538: 'Bellmontes Lease sumtyme a great park by Leicester but now converted to pasture.' During the reign of Henry's daughter Elizabeth I, the rate of pasturage in Beaumont Leys from May Day until Lammas (1 August) was 3s 2d for the poor and 4s 2d for the rich. The charge for the horse of a poor man to graze the land was 3d and 4d for his wealthier neighbours, but where the demarcation line for wealth and poverty was is not clear. The revenue from the sparse population in the area would have been very small.

Beaumont Leys House in the summer of 1889. A small boy with a round cap is in the lush meadow in front of the Queen Anne house, which became part of the Home Farm complex.

During the 18th century Beaumont Leys comprised three farms, the largest being about 400 acres. Some time at the end of the 17th century and the beginning of the 18th Beaumont Leys passed to John Aislabie (1670–1742) who became Chancellor of the Exchequer in 1714. Aislabie achieved a certain amount of notoriety for his part in the South Sea Bubble affair. Even King George I was not immune as two of his mistresses were involved the scandal. As a director of the South Sea Company with high parliamentary office, Aislabie was instrumental in the passing of the South Sea Act in 1720 and was imprisoned in the Tower of London. It is suggested that the red chequered brick, gabled manor house known as Beaumont Leys House, with its local Swithland slate roof, was built in the late 17th century, possibly by Aislabie. It was also during his tenure that extensive planting took place, avenues of elm, together with clusters of oak and elm trees in the centre of each field. In 1699 Aislabie also inherited the Studley Royal Estate in North Yorkshire. He was something of a gentleman landscape gardener and skilfully designed the gardens with temples, water features and a view of the ruins of nearby Fountains Abbey.

Beaumont Leys Lodge, 1889. The elegant classically proportioned house, with its fashionable monkey puzzle tree, became the Neighbourhood Centre in Astill Lodge Road.

Early in the 19th century the Ellis family began their association with Beaumont Leys. John Ellis moved from Beighton in Derbyshire to Sharmans Lodge, near Leicester, and he then took the tenancy of Beaumont Leys farm. By this time the house was surrounded by elms, walnuts and limes and no one can express more eloquently than Eliza Ellis, John's daughter, in *Letters and Memorials of Eliza Ellis*, 'the carpet of soft turf, the pure fragrant air'. Margaret Ellis (who compiled the book) also remembered the many hard-working Irish men who came to reap the corn every summer and how in the depression of 1826 agricultural workers went to bed early to save candles.

The Ellis children, who appeared to enjoy a carefree childhood, also christened the large pool near the house 'the moat'. The pool or large pond was a source of constant enjoyment, on which toy boats were sailed in summer, and there was sliding on the ice in winter. The neighbouring farm was called 'The Stocking'; during the Napoleonic Wars (1793–1815) the oaks were felled to supply timber to the navy. There was also Stocking Wood, which the 18th-century historian John Nichols noted was the site of a rare wild flower. The name continues in the Stocking Farm Estate.

In 1830 Beaumont Leys was listed as an extra parochial part of the hundreds of Sparkenhoe and West Goscote. It consisted of seven acres of land, which contained two houses and 14 inhabitants. The sole proprietor of the land was Miss Lawrence, the granddaughter of the former Chancellor, John Aislabie. She died in 1844 and the estate passed to Admiral Cornwallis Ricketts. It was during John Ellis's time at Beaumont Leys that he was approached by William Stenson, of Longlane Colliery, Whitwick, with the idea of a railway between Leicester and Swannington. He decided to visit the engineer and inventor George Stephenson, who had already built the famous *Rocket* (1829) and *Comet* (1832) engines. Stephenson was a busy man and could only be persuaded to discuss the railway after '… a beefsteak dinner at a local inn.' Well replete after his meal he agreed but suggested his son Robert should manage the project. George Stephenson used his influence to raise money in Liverpool for the work to be carried out – he felt that this would repay the many Leicester people who had invested heavily in the canals. John Ellis became director of the Midland Railway, as well as the Leicester Swannington Railway and in 1845 became Chairman of the Midland Counties Railway. Because of his many commitments he decided it would be better to leave his son Alfred to manage the farm and seek a new home elsewhere. The Ellis family had lived at Beaumont Leys for nearly 40 years. Alfred and his wife Lucy continued to farm at Beaumont Leys until 1849, when they left to join the rest of the family, who had moved to Belgrave.

Cornwallis Ricketts died in 1885 and Sir Robert Tempest became the new owner. In

Christmas shopping in 1986.

the same year Sir Robert sold 100 acres of his land to Leicester Corporation and leased almost all of the remainder (1,260 acres) for the next 30 years. Desperate overcrowding due to the huge increase in the population of Leicester in the latter half of the 19th century led the Corporation to seek improved methods of sewage disposal. The site at Beaumont Leys was ideal and in 1901 the corporation purchased the remainder of the Beaumont Leys Estate from the Tempest family. The sparsely populated farmland was an invitation to poachers and the front page of the *Leicester Advertiser* on 26 January 1895 reported that two men were summonsed for poaching with nets on farmland at Beaumont Leys, but it does not record their fate. Farming continued until well into the 20th century and the entire site became known as the City Farms; the sewage works finally closed in 1964.

There were seven farms in all, the buildings of four of which survive in some form: Home Farm Neighbourhood Centre, comprised of parts of Beaumont Leys House and Home Farm, Beaumont Lodge, Birstall Lodge Farm and Glebe Lodge. In the 1930s cattle, said to be of the highest quality, sheep and poultry were the main types of livestock, together with arable farming. During World War Two, the Home Guard used Beaumont Leys House as their headquarters. The buildings did not escape damage during the war, as a bomb that fell in the nearby Abbey Lane area caused windows to shatter.

Beaumont Leys began to be developed for housing and industrial estates in the early 1970s. The original plans incorporated a monorail link between the new development

An aerial view, 1985.

The rear of Beaumont Leys Lodge, with its many outbuildings in a dilapidated state in 1984, when the grade II listed building was being considered for use as a neighbourhood centre.

Young trees and shrubs in leafy Grassington Close in the spring of 1987.

and the city centre, but this was not carried out. A possible lake for watersports was also planned, causing great concern to residents in the nearby village of Anstey. The *Leicester Mercury* of 18 January 1967 records that villagers thought they might be encroached upon by the city and become 'some soulless suburbia'. Housing, begun in 1972, much of it to the designs of Alan Watson (who was to become the City Architect in 1973), was a mixture of municipal and private, with the involvement of a number of housing associations. Although there is a large mass of housing, there are few high buildings and a variety of styles and materials are used. Red, orange and beige brickwork, weatherboarding and dense planting of shrubs prevents this from being a bleak area. There were initial problems due to a lack of amenities and vandalism but despite this most residents liked the landscaped open green spaces. The *Leicester Mercury* of 26 June 1980 quoted one homeowner: '... On a nice morning it's like waking up on holiday.' On 22 June 1983 a new church was consecrated. In August 1993, the *Leicester Mercury* reported on the dearth of public houses in an area almost exactly the same size as Market Harborough: the latter could boast 15 whereas Beaumont Leys had only two. Even the busy shopping centre had only a third as many shops as can be found in Market Harborough.

In the 21st century Beaumont Leys has a lively, youthful community and although it cannot hope to quite recapture the delightful countryside the Ellis family enjoyed in the

An idyllic avenue of trees on Glovers Walk, 1987.

The countryside in suburbia: fields between Krefeld Way and Bennion Road, summer 1983.

19th century it is still a surprisingly green area of the city. There are many lawns and trees, and not many public libraries can boast a lawn complete with flowerbeds as you approach the entrance! For all its modernity the area can also has a surprising amount of hidden history.

Further Reading:

Brown, C., J. Mills and B. Jarrett, *Beaumont Leys and Home Farm*, Home Farm Neighbourhood Centre, 1997.

Ellis, M., *Letters and Memorials of Eliza Ellis*, privately published, 1883.

Tura, E., *A Roman Occupation Site Castle Hill-Beaumont Leys*, published by the author, 1986

BELGRAVE

Merdegrave was the original name for Belgrave, meaning 'marten grove'. Some have suggested that the meaning was 'dirty wood' and that over the years the name Belgrave came into use, which meant 'beautiful or fine wood'. From the time of William I in 1066 the name Belgrave was in use, although some have claimed that the name only came into use in 1227. There are rather more mythical suggestions that the name is derived from a weighty bell that was left at Belgrave, as it was too heavy to continue on its journey to another village. More widely known is the story of Bel the giant, who declared he could reach Leicester with three mighty leaps on his horse. The following anonymous verse explains his unfortunate journey:

Mountsorrel he mounted at,
Rothley he rode by,
Wanlip he leaped o'er,
Birstall he burst his gall,
At Belgrave he was buried at.

The parish of Belgrave, 1½ miles north-east of Leicester, was originally in the East Goscote hundred. It also contained the chapelries of Birstall and south Thurmaston. The

An old cottage and St Peter's Church from the river.

St Peter's Church, Church Road.

civil parish of Belgrave transferred to Leicester in 1892 and the remainder, which had become part of Beaumont Leys, came to Leicester in 1935. In 1830, when it included Birstall and south Thurmaston, it contained 3,750 acres of land, on which stood 372 houses with 1,904 inhabitants, most of whom were employed in the framework knitting industry.

In 1086 the major landowner in Belgrave was Hugh de Grentemesnil, who held seven caracutes (about 700 acres) of land. His wife Adeliz held a further caracute. In 1204 the earldom of Leicester was divided along with that of Belgrave. Simon de Montfort had one portion and Saer de Quency the other. The land was held by custodians as de Montfort's English possessions were taken by King John after the First Barons War against him. Belgrave was returned to Simon the younger by Henry III. Simon de Montfort's associations with Leicester (although it is doubtful he ever set foot in the town) are commemorated in his statue on the clock tower, De Montfort Hall and De Montfort University.

The origins of a church in Belgrave existed prior to 1081, when it was granted with its tithes and eleven virginates to the Norman abbey of St Evroul (Orne) by Hugh de Grentemesnil. In the Middle Ages Belgrave was one of the more substantial livings in the county. Increases continued to be given to the incumbents and in 1831 the stipend was valued at £154. By 1847 this had almost doubled to £300.

The present church of St Peter, together with its large churchyard, is situated in a picturesque leafy enclave, which includes Belgrave Hall and Belgrave House. The church has a fine Norman south doorway. W.G. Hoskins refers to it as: '… the best Norman doorway in the country'. Other elements of the building date from the 12th century, but the main part is from the 13th century, with a 19th-century chancel. The uppermost part of the tower and clerestory date from the 16th century. Early in the 19th century Birstall parish, being a chapel of ease to Belgrave, generously supplied new gates to the church. On a more domestic note the Revd G. Boulter replanted his orchard with 20 apple and pear trees. There were numerous repairs and alterations throughout the centuries but the church has still retained much of its original structure. In the 19th century work was carried out by Ewan Christian in 1860 and Sir George Gilbert Scott in 1877–8. Scott designed and restored several churches in the city and county but his most famous national work, more well known than the churches and even more well used, is St Pancras Station and Hotel, London.

A postcard from Belgrave with views of St Peter's Church, cottages, Belgrave House, the Talbot Inn and trams near the school.

Belgrave churchyard has a tall, ornate monument to Joseph Cave, who lived in Victoria Road, Belgrave. He died on 6 August 1921. What is unusual about his tombstone is that he had it erected some nine years before his death. He apparently hated anything that was done quickly and decided to make his funeral arrangements well in advance. He sat on a seat in the churchyard, in quiet contemplation, overseeing his grave being dug. When the operation was complete he joined the gravediggers, giving them a rendition of the song: *Poor Old Joe.* A smoke and a conversation with the men completed the day's events and Joe was happy in the knowledge that his eventual funeral would not be the usual rushed affair. Vicarage Lane no longer leads to the early 19th-century rectory, which was demolished in 1964. It retains a pleasant row of late 19th-century villas, named after the villages within a few miles of Belgrave. Some of these retain their decorative leaded windows. Despite the tranquil setting the visitor is reminded of the 21st century by the large yellow police notice warning motorists to beware of thieves.

The red-brick church of St Michael and all Angels on Belgrave Road, designed by George Vialls, was built in 1885–7, to serve the increasing population of the expanding village. Prior to this a temporary iron church had served the community from 1878.

Roman Catholicism held sway in Belgrave from the late 17th century and it is suggested that the village played a major part in the Roman Catholic revival in Leicester. The old Belgrave Hall, home of the Byerley family, housed a Roman Catholic chapel, and they had their own Franciscan chaplain from the late 17th century to the early 18th

Belgrave recreation ground, c.1930.

century. In 1790 John Throsby wrote that Mr Denshire, the son of a Leicester Alderman, lived: 'in an old mansion, adjoining to which once stood a Catholic Chapel'. Other reports suggest that it survived until the early 1800s, when it fell into disuse. Throsby also recounts the amusing tale of the 'deaf and dumb beggar' who knocked on the door of the old hall, to be greeted by Mr Byerley, 'who was but little in stature, but he lacked not discernment.' He provided the beggar with a substantial meal and then enquired of him how long he had been deaf and dumb. At the prompt reply of 'seven years,' Byerley ordered his coachman to 'flog the rascal from my yard'.

The site of the old Belgrave Hall, owned by the Hastings and then the Byerley families, is reputed to be on the site of the former Constitutional Club on Loughborough Road. Until this was altered in the 1990s a window from the chapel was still to be seen in the north wall of the building. The building is now used for educational tuition. In 1709, 18 of the 60 families living in Belgrave were Roman Catholic. Despite the history of Roman Catholicism in Belgrave it was to be a further 200 years before the Roman Catholics in the area received a place of worship, when in 1922 the Chapel of Our Lady was consecrated. Nonconformity in the area was represented by the Baptists and Methodists, who had a number of chapels consecrated in the 19th century.

The present Belgrave Hall was built between 1709 and 1713 for Edmond and Ann Craddock. Their initials and dates are still to be seen on the rainwater heads. The building

The old school, with the police sergeant's house opposite.

has a plain, almost severe façade to Church Road, but this is offset with interesting chequered brickwork and some very fine wrought iron gates, contemporary with the house. By about 1740 the house was owned by William Vann, who was later to become High Sheriff of Leicestershire. It remained in the family until 1844, when the last Mrs Vann died. A charming tradition is recorded that on Valentines Day, the village children would apparently visit Mrs Vann to sing a Valentine rhyme, after which they were rewarded with pennies and buns.

If you've got a penny in your pocket
Slip it into mine
We used to come at eight o'clock
But now we come at nine.

In 1776 William Vann decided to build a new house across the road, the elegant Belgrave House. William and Ann moved in and other members of the family lived at Belgrave Hall. Like Belgrave Hall the Vann family owned Belgrave House until the 19th century, after which it passed through various hands. An advertisement was placed in the *Leicester Journal* of 14 October 1852 for the house to be let, declaring among other things that it was: 'A residence suitable for a gentleman' and a 'beautiful mansion-like dwelling, situated at Belgrave, near Leicester'. The property was purchased by the Corporation for £3,000 on 21 December 1936 and was used as a temporary day nursery for 19 years. It is presently used by Leicester Museum and Art Gallery. At the other end of the spectrum, the poor were catered for by the addition of a small workhouse in the 18th century.

Bemused villagers regard the floodwater on the Green, while children happily paddle.

Education in Belgrave consisted of two Anglican Sunday schools in 1832, the earliest being opened in 1787. The National School was built in 1836, with the addition of an infant's school in 1848, which received much support from the Ellis family of Belgrave Hall. John Ellis, who was chairman of the Midland Counties Railway, had bought the hall in 1845. John Ellis and his family first went to view Belgrave Hall in February 1845. His daughter Eliza describes it as ghostly: 'The white hall and staircase had a ghostly hue...', and she goes on to mention the two old servants who were left to guard the '... silent rooms'. What Eliza Ellis could not have known is that ghosts are still a major topic of conversation at Belgrave Hall today, with suggested sightings of a lady in Victorian dress.

In the 1840s framework knitting still remained the only trade of the area. Eliza notes that many of the 'stockingers' were well read. Perhaps the well-educated knitters were the inspiration for the small village library, which opened on 16 October 1852. The industrious Eliza had stamped and numbered all the books, with hopes of purchasing more and increasing membership. The Ellis family lived here until John Ellis's last daughter, Mary, died in 1923. After a relatively brief ownership by T.A. Morley, Leicester Corporation opened it as a museum in 1937. The family of Thomas Morley and Son (Hosiery Manufacturers) had lived in Belgrave in the 1880s, and Thomas's second son Harry was born there in 1881. Harry was to become an artist of note. As a nine-year-old

A wintry day on Claremont Street. The off-license on the opposite corner to the Methodist Church advertises Fry's Chocolate and Brunt and Co. Ltd, Celebrated Wooden Boxed Ales.

he had attended watercolour classes in Belgrave, given by William Barrow. After attending the Royal College of Art, it had been his intention to become an architect. Despite winning many awards and being articled to a major Edwardian architect, the lure of the canvas was too great and he returned to his first love of painting. Belgrave Hall is now furnished and decorated as it would have been in the early 18th century, and its extensive and elegant gardens are open to all. The museum also houses a fine collection of furniture designed by Ernest Gimson (1863–1926).

There were various water mills in Belgrave over the centuries, and one survived in working order until 1895. In 1846 John Tempest was the mill owner, and he leased the mill some time prior to 1863 to William Evans, who had a corn-milling business. In 1863 his daughter Isabel was born and spent her early childhood living in the mill house. She recalled what a wonderful place it was for children, despite falling in the stream! The garden had a croquet lawn at one end with a border of lavender bushes and a weeping ash at the other. In the lively imagination of Isabel and her siblings the tree often became a 'summer house' or 'brigand's castle'. Isabel's cousin Mary wrote of the wonderful swing, from which 'it was our delight to jump into the waiting arms of numerous young men who came to the Mill House.' The Evans children received 1d a week pocket money, which they would save up to spend on 'chocolate creams, coconut

Children in a variety of hats play near the 16th-century cottage, 16 April 1904.

Girls pose outside Belgrave Hall, while the boys look idly on, 18 April 1904.

Belgrave School.

candy, and ginger-beer-with-a-straw'. These delights would then be devoured on top of a haystack.

Isabel Evans (later Ellis) remembered a number of Belgrave residents from the 1860s, most of whom lived on the Leicester Road. These included Mrs Henry, 'a very beautiful, stately old lady' who lived at Elm Cottage. At the Beeches lived the Wright family, who each year had a most wonderful Christmas tree. Little girls at their Christmas parties were given exquisitely dressed china-headed dolls from the tree. Next door to the Beeches was the Grange, the home of the elderly Mrs Thompson. Mrs Thompson drove a brougham to Belvoir Street Chapel every Sunday, and occasionally the young Isabel was allowed to travel with her and share 'the glories of her Brougham'. Mrs Ellis also recalled the Belgrave mummers visiting Belgrave Hall at Christmas time. They played the parts of various characters, including St George and the dragon.

A most important building in Belgrave is the Talbot Inn, reputed to have 14th-century origins. The earliest innkeepers recorded are Henry and Mary Dawson, who were married locally by special license. The parish records of 1784 note some extensive alterations: 'the parish house known by the name of the Talbot Inn was new built in the front by Mr Wm Glover, the tenant, the expense being about 270 pounds'. Its present façade is the result of alterations in 1958, when the third storey was unfortunately removed and the bricks roughcast rendered. The 18th century in Belgrave also saw the 'great frost' of 1740 and over 50 years later there were hardships for the poor when corn and meat were 'excessively dear'.

It was during the 18th century that Belgrave began to develop as a suburb of Leicester. Although transport was still very limited, repairs and alterations to Belgrave Bridge in the second half of the century made Leicester more accessible. A new bridge was opened in 1835, designed by Leicester architect, William Parsons. In 1791 canals were dug to the north and south of the village, enabling barges to transport goods. A number of wealthy Leicester tradesmen acquired residences in Belgrave and the rapidly developing hosiery industry began to make an impact on the village. In 1801 the population was 601, with only 55 people working on the land. Almost three times as many were craftspeople or were employed in trade and industry. Thirty years later, in 1831, framework-knitters comprised most of the population. Socks were apparently the main articles produced. Despite the encroachment of industry Belgrave was still very much a village in the 1850s, the nucleus of houses and cottages being close to St Peter's Church and in Bath Street. Before the development of Stoneygate the area was also attractive to Leicester businessmen, particularly those in the hosiery trade. In the mid 19th-century it was variously home to William Fielding, Thomas Angrave, Alfred Donisthorpe and many others. There were only a few houses on Loughborough Road and Abbey Lane and Melton Road had fields to either side.

In the last 30 years of the 19th century suburbanisation was rapid and the population had increased to 12,000 by 1900. Gas lighting reached the village in 1864 and a horse-drawn tram service commenced operating from Christmas Eve 1874, to serve the expanding village. Prior to this a horse bus had operated several times a week. When the new tram service came into operation the fare was 2d from Belgrave to the Clock Tower and it was the cause of great excitement. An experimental steam tram was tried on the Belgrave route in 1876, 'Hughes Patent Steam Tramway', but it could not compete with the horse trams and was withdrawn. To quote a conversation between two working-class women heard by Isabel Ellis in the early days of the horse trams: 'I had 2s 6d for a holiday, and I spent it sitting in the tram 'til it was all gone.' It was probably considered just as thrilling as a day at a bank holiday fair! One such fair took place in Belgrave on Wake Monday, at the beginning of July.

The town of Leicester was growing continually and from the 1860s Belgrave Road and Melton Road became lined with streets of red-brick terraced houses. In 1877 land previously owned by Isaac Harrison of Newfoundpool House was sold to William Gray and subsequently purchased by the Leicester Freehold Land Society.

Leicester architects Shenton and Baker drew up plans for five roads on the 11-acre site: Harrison, Gipsy, Moores, Flax and Arbor Roads. The land sold for £1,300 per acre and John Lea of Charles Street submitted the cheapest tender of £2,310 to make up the roads. By 1891 Loughborough Road had many fine houses, many of which were tall elegant villas set well back from the road. The following year Belgrave became part of the borough of Leicester. In 1904 electric trams came into use to serve the expanding suburban population and the Belgrave route was used to test one of the new trams.

By the time the new electric tram route was inaugurated in 1904 most of the area was built up. Cossington Street Library, the swimming baths, where you could also have a bath, as very few houses in the area had bathrooms, and the recreation ground were built to serve the large population. Arthur Wakerley's rather pleasing Wesleyan Hall, always known locally as Belgrave Hall, was added in 1898. The Belgrave cinema, designed by Seale and Riley, notable Leicester architects who designed a number of cinemas, opened in 1913. It had virtually a captive audience as it stood opposite the giant Union Works of the British United Shoe Machinery Company, which employed 6,000 people. Just along from the cinema the Leicester Co-operative Society had a row of shops and a café. Belgrave Road was and still is a busy commercial area. Today it is

The Talbot Inn in the 1950s before it was altered, with a 1949 car parked outside.

Checketts Road at the beginning of the 20th century. The corner shop sign reads 'J. Patrick, Proprietor, Hay, Straw and Corn Merchant'. A barber's pole hangs from a shop further down and a sign for the Co-op is painted on the side of a wall, just below the roofline.

known as 'The Golden Mile', and many notable Asian shops and restaurants are to be found there. In the early 1960s many Kenyan Asians arrived in Leicester, followed by others expelled from Uganda in the 1970s, and they began to make their homes in the Belgrave Road area. In the ensuing decades Belgrave Road has become synonymous with delicious Indian food and beautiful fabrics are available from the many sari shops. The whole area is lively and diverse, particularly on occasions like Diwali, when the entire road is decorated with colourful lights. The area holds the largest Diwali in Europe.

The Church of England primary school, built in 1861 of Mountsorrel granite, finally closed its doors in 1974. The *Leicester Mercury* of 19 February 1974 reported that it was the oldest school building in Leicester. The clock on the Thurcaston Road façade of the building, bought to commemorate Queen Victoria's jubilee of 1887, still keeps perfect time. The building is now used for commercial purposes. In the early part of the 20th century Belgrave housed a home for mentally ill girls and in 1929 the 18th-century house known as Cross Corners was similarly used for boys. The house is now in the process of being transformed into an arts centre for the community and Mellor Community Primary School.

A corner shop on the Loughborough Road in the late 19th century, with the name 'A. Lucas' above the door. The plethora of advertisements include: Barr's Tea, Nestle's Swiss Milk, Fry's and Cadbury's Chocolate, Coleman's Mustard and starch. The London Daily Chronicle *and the* Daily Telegraph *are on sale and telegrams can be sent for a penny.*

The centre of Belgrave still retains a tranquil village atmosphere. Despite the sadly boarded up windows on the garden front, the elegance and splendour of Belgrave House still remain. Throsby, in 1790, delighted in this corner of Belgrave: 'the glittering stream, the lofty bank and trees ... the sloping pleasure ground of the Vanns, all on the same side; and on the other you behold a valley, rich with flowers of golden and variegated tints'. R.G. Waddington, writing in *The Illustrated Leicester Chronicle*, 4 April 1931, declares it: '... a delightful old-world area that cannot be beaten in the neighbourhood of Leicester.' It has changed little since Waddington or even Throsby was singing its praises; even some of the view is still afforded. The small close is also something of a time capsule of architectural history.

Further reading:

Couchman, E. (Ed.), *Belgrave as I Remember It*, Leicestershire Libraries and Information Service, 1984.
Ellis, I.C., *Nineteenth Century Leicester*, published by the author, 1935.
Lee, J., *Who's Buried Where in Leicestershire*, Leicestershire Libraries and Information Service, 1991.

Three elderly ladies chatting in the backyard, viewed through the 16th-century gateway.

Melton Road, with a tram climbing the hill, c.1920.

Cross Corners, Thurcaston Road, in the late 19th century. An advertisement for twice-nightly shows at the Palace Theatre in Belgrave Gate is posted on a building further along the road.

The Old Bridge, with two boys in the meadow below, 12 June 1900.

Belgrave Road in the 1900s with elegant Art Nouveau tram overhead wire standards. The well-stocked newsagents, built in 1868, advertises the News of the World *and Cambo cigarettes.*

The south side of the Old Soar Bridge, 18 April 1904.

St Peter's churchyard.

The Green.

A young girl beside the 16th-century cottages.

David Ward's house, Berridge Lane, c.1906.

The Talbot Inn.

Cattle grazing in Belgrave Meadows, with the rear of Belgrave House in the distance.

A wintry day in Elmdale Street in the 1920s with the coalman on his round.

Ladies on their doorsteps in Bath Street. A tall factory chimney in the distance is a sign of the industrial expansion of Leicester.

Melton Road in the 1900s. The Midland Hotel is the taller building on the right, while the shops are W.M. Cant, family butcher, at No.179, and J.H. Walker, drapers, at No.181 on the corner.

Thurcaston Road in the early 20th century. The café on the right also advertises boats for hire. As well as the usual Cadbury's Cocoa sign, there is a board saying: 'Try Spencer's Hop Beer and Lemon Pop, 4d and 1d.'

Men looking over the Old Bridge, probably some time in the 1930s.

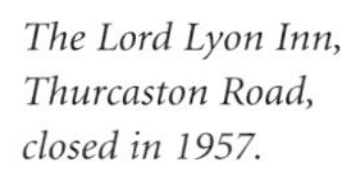

The Lord Lyon Inn, Thurcaston Road, closed in 1957.

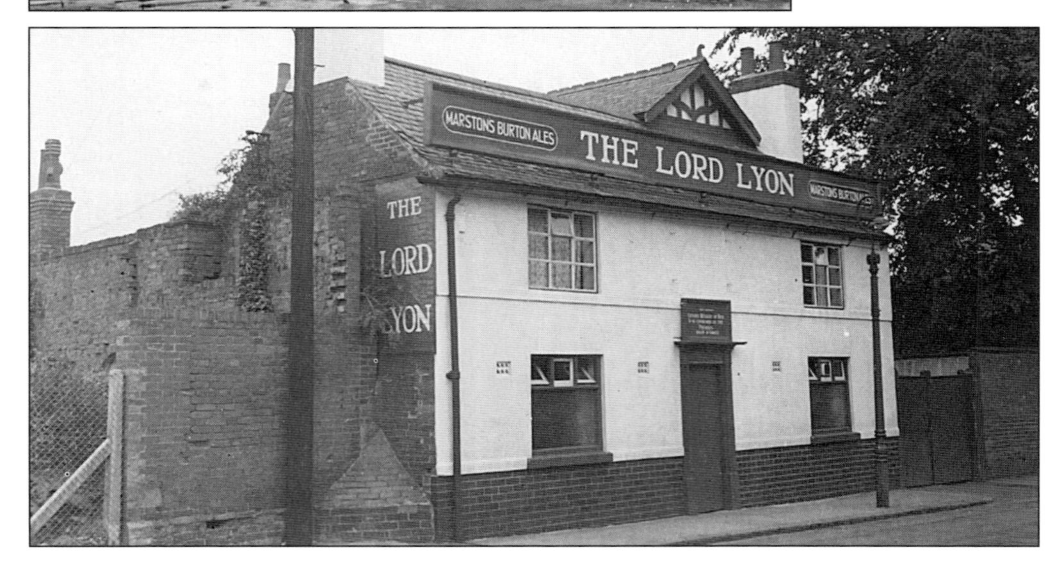

The old vicarage, sadly being demolished in 1964.

The Talbot and Lord Lyon Inns, 1951.

A thatched cottage in Bath Street in 1951. Despite the rural air a fairly early television aerial sprouts from the thatch.

Thurcaston Road bridge, 1912.

The rear of Belgrave House, with an early 20th-century extension to the left.

The front of Belgrave Hall, taken from the gardens of Belgrave House.

Belgrave Tollgate, c.1870. A wagonload of hay passes through. Although it is summer and one lady has a parasol, the other wears a pale fur-trimmed coat.

There is nothing new about large class sizes, as this photograph of children at Belgrave National School in 1915 indicates.

The Belgrave Laundry Company, Dyers and Cleaners, established in 1872 in Laundry Lane. Harry Veall is the driver and his son Dick (John Harry) is the small boy on the footboard. The van boy is either Dick Weston, who was there from 1903–4, or Bill Flint who held the post in 1906.

W. Cooper's, No.237 Melton Road, on the corner of St Michael's Avenue. Staff pose with a horse and cart, piled high with all kinds of tools, hardware and household goods. The board declares: 'Picture Framing, Lowest "Phore" Prices.'

Another view of W. Cooper's Hardware and Petroleum Stores, Ironmongers and General House Furnishers, at No.237 Melton Road on the corner of St Michael's Avenue. The tin trunks cost from 3s 6d 'Cheap' to 9s 6d 'Large Size'. The 'Baby Size' can be had for 4s 6d and the one for 8s 6d is labelled 'Good Value'. The saucepans ranged from 1s 2d to 3s 9d.

The front of Belgrave House.

Laying rails for the new electric trams at Melton Turn, 1903–4. A large gang of workmen are employed using only primitive tools. The nearby horse tram carries advertisements for Bovril, the Palace Theatre and a garden fête.

The rear of Belgrave House with a couple at the centre ground floor window, c.1850.

Checketts Road, 1961. Belgrave Shoe Repairs are to the left and the local branch of Worthington's can be seen on the Loughborough Road, next door to Urcell's.

Braunstone

Braunstone, Brantestone, Brant's or Brand's (there are many variations) is recorded in the Domesday Book of 1086. Its tenant in chief was Hugh de Grentemesnil, who held a little under 5½ caracutes of land (a caracute is approximately 100 acres). William the Conqueror had given him the land, together with many other manors in Leicestershire. Among other early landowners was Margaret de Ferrers in the second half of the 13th century: her descendants, who lived in Groby, were to remain in possession of Braunstone until the death of William, Lord Ferrers, in 1445. The Grey family of Groby, associated with Lady Jane Grey, then held the land until 1554. Later the Hastings family became associated with Braunstone and Henry Hastings is reputed to have had the manor house built in around 1600. Hastings later became financially impoverished supporting the Royalist cause in the Civil War. There are also suggestions that there was a manor prior to this built in the late 13th century. Several farm buildings including a barn, complete with a dovecote in the gable, survived until at least the 1950s. The church of St Peter, although of 12th-century origin, is much altered. Restoration work was carried out on the tower in 1704 and a brick porch was added in 18th century. The church was extended considerably in 1937 to cope with the growing suburb, and further alterations were carried out in 1972. The village is 2¼ miles south-west of Leicester.

The family most closely associated with Braunstone were the Winstanleys, who were to remain in possession for 275 years. James Winstanley purchased the manor in 1650 for £6,000 from Fernando Hastings. James was a lawyer and Puritan and in his capacity as Recorder of Leicester proclaimed Oliver Cromwell Lord Protector. In 1662 his anti-

The smithy as depicted on a postcard shortly before World War One.

The bridle lane to Lubbesthorpe in the county part of Braunstone, 1963.

parliamentarian views forced him to relinquish his post. In the mid-18th century the estate was inherited by his great-great-grandson, also called James, who held the office of High Sheriff of Leicester. Some time in 1750 James decided to tunnel for coal, close to what are now the lakes on Braunstone Park. After a fortnight of intensive investigations by the estate workers, the site was vandalised overnight, with suspicion falling on other colliers in the county. John Throsby, writing in 1790, noted: 'This piece of villainy so disconcerted the views of a praise-worthy character, the late Mr Winstanley, that he made no farther attempts to find coals.' In the same year as his mining experiment in 1750, James Winstanley was also busy renewing some of his tenant's leases: these also show the extent of the Winstanley estate. One of James's tenants, John Johnson, who had his lease renewed for the next nine years, lived on Braunstone Lane, near the Rowley Fields. He had a cottage: '... with a stable and

A house on Braunstone Lane, photographed in 1935.

Braunstone Lane, 1927.

brewhouse consisting of 5 bays of building, also a little garden on the south side of the Rowley Fields.'

James's son Clement inherited the estate on his father's death in 1770 and six years later had the hall built. It was designed in a pleasant understated Classical style by Leicester architect and builder, James Oldham, who was to be Lord Mayor of Leicester in

Narborough Road and the corner of Coalpit Lane, January 1930. The road from Braunstone is in the foreground.

The smithy.

1783. The three-storey Hall is red brick with stone dressings. Its construction was not without mishap, the building claiming the lives of a stonemason and labourer. Many others were seriously injured when scaffolding collapsed. These tragic events gave rise to theories of ghosts at the hall. A number of ghostly figures have been noted over the years including black horses (almost always used for funerals), spirited away with their carriages in the eerie spinney at night. The melancholy figures of a boy at a window, a

The smithy in the 1920s. The long low sports car is an Arrol-Johnson, made in Glasgow.

The thatched cottage home of Edward Jones, blacksmith and parish clerk in 1863.

groom who took his own life and a girl in white, thought to be a novice nun who sadly died of tuberculosis in 1899, at the age of 18, are also seen. In 1898, Richard Winstanley's two sisters, May aged 17 and Georgina aged 19, became Roman Catholic novice nuns at the convent of the Order of the Sacred Heart. Within a year May had died and it is she who is thought to wander the corridors of Braunstone Hall. Numerous other eerie figures are thought to inhabit the hall, but unfortunately they have not been terrifying enough to deter the vandals, who also appear during the night.

A further tragedy that affected the family was the disappearance of James Beaumont Winstanley, who inherited the estate in 1855. He was another Winstanley to hold the office of High Sheriff of Leicester. During a trip to Europe in 1862, much to the consternation of his family in Leicestershire, he appeared to vanish. After a body had been discovered in the Moselle River at Coblenz in Germany, his family, fearing the worst, sent out the Leicester private detective 'Tanky Smith' to investigate. Smith, in the company of a butler from Braunstone Hall, was able to identify cufflinks and clothing and thus confirm that it was the body of the missing High Sheriff.

James Beaumont Winstanley was the last of the male line of the Winstanley family to hold the estate. The estate then passed to his sister, Anna Jane, who was married to Ralph Pochin. Their descendants then took the name of Winstanley. It was during one harsh winter of their tenure that the *Leicester Advertiser* of 26 January 1895 noted that 'The poor of Braunstone were given 5cwt of coals by Mr W.T. Blastock, taken to every cottage by Mr Clarke and Mr Tilley.' In 1904 Anna gave up the estate to her son Richard, who

Narborough Road, May 1929, looking towards Meredith Road. A Rover 8 is in the distance.

Narborough Road, May 1929, looking towards the city. There are a number of cyclists and to the right a bull-nosed Morris car.

Narborough Road and Coalpit Lane, May 1929. Braunstone Estate is in the background. The women are fashionably dressed in knee-length coats, cloche hats and ankle strap shoes.

extended the hall in 1911 to include more modern amenities. His initials and those of his wife Kitty are incorporated into the decorative brickwork. Major Winstanley also had two small lodges added before World War One, designed by Leicester architect Ralph Waldo Bedingfield (1872–1940).

The Winstanleys were only able to enjoy life at Braunstone Hall for another 14 years. In the aftermath of World War One, vast amounts of land were required to fulfil the need to provide more and better quality housing. In 1924 Leicester Corporation sought to compulsorily purchase land in Braunstone from Major Richard Winstanley. Major Winstanley was understandably extremely reluctant to dispose of the estate which had been held by his family for nearly three centuries and it was only after lengthy negotiations that the sale went through. The Leicester Corporation minutes for 1925 record that the estate, consisting of 1,064 acres, Rose Farm, Gallards Hill Farm, Braunstone Frith Farm, Hockley Hole Farm, Old Hall Farm, New Fields Farm, parsonage, school house, blacksmith's shop and 15 cottages, including one in ruins, were purchased for £115,000. The cottages on Main Street and Cressida Place were designed in 1858 and 1859 by William Butterfield, an architect of national importance. The cottages were an early form of what was to become known as the Domestic Revival style and much of the housing on Braunstone Estate is based on this style.

Considering the expansion of Leicester and the suburbanisation of many other parts

Sports Corner café at the corner of Coalpit Lane and Narborough Road, May 1929. A new privately built detached house is on the right.

of the borough it was remarkable that Braunstone remained a small agricultural village well into the 20th century. From 1801–1881 the population remained at an average of 200 people. From the 1880s until 1911 the population declined considerably as the result of a lengthy agricultural depression. There were also many more shoe and hosiery factories in Leicester, which with better hours and pay attracted workers from villages just over the borough boundary. Some factories were conveniently situated in Western Road, not more than a mile and a half from the village towards Leicester. By the 1900s there were also many more houses off of the Narborough and Hinckley Roads to attract people who had previously lived in the countryside.

Many of the buildings in Braunstone were of an early date and only a few were added in the 19th century. Funded by James Winstanley, the parsonage was built in 1864 and the National School, complete with schoolhouse, was erected in 1868. It is quite likely that Catherine Furborough was the first qualified teacher at the school: she was there from about 1871 until 1900. The 18th-century Old Hall farmhouse was still standing in the early 1950s and an article in the *Leicester Mercury*, 23 January 1952, noted that it was unaltered and still lit by oil lamps. The writer went on to say 'I noticed the late tenant has surrendered to one necessity, a wireless set, but he had not discarded a box mangle.' Many generations of the Johnson family had occupied the house, the aunt of the last tenant reaching 101 before she died in 1943. The building was finally demolished to make way for a housing estate in the early 1970s.

Building began on municipal housing in 1926 and by 1928 £379,000 had been spent

Narborough Road, 1926, looking towards the city. A Standard car is parked on the right. New Fields farmhouse on the left used to sell country produce to the public and was just outside the borough boundary in Braunstone parish, almost opposite Somerville Road.

Narborough Road South in the 1960s.

on housing. By 1931 the population had reached 7,000, bringing about enormous change to a village which in 1921 had a population of 238. In 1935 a considerable part of the parish of Braunstone became part of the city of Leicester, having formerly been a chapelry of Glenfield. Braunstone still remains divided between the city and the county. From 1935 to 1937, 1,000 further houses were added in North Braunstone. These were provided to rehouse people from the inner-city areas, which were being redeveloped to provide better roads and housing close to the city centre. The area was designed with a

The old village school.

garden suburb layout, providing space and greenery. Braunstone Hall opened as a senior school in 1932 and the following year became a junior school as families with younger children continued to move into the area.

During World War Two, in the autumn of 1940, Braunstone had its share of alarm and excitement when a young German pilot made a forced landing in a field close to Dunstall Avenue. The charming blonde pilot, who spoke excellent English, was discovered by a group of housewives armed with only kitchen knives and garden tools. The daughter of one of these ladies, writing in the *Leicester Mercury* of 21 February 2003, recalls that they were so captivated by his very pleasing manner that not only was he provided with a cup of tea but the ladies insisted that he was treated well by the army and police when they arrived to remove him.

In 1933 the Roxy Cinema opened its doors to the inhabitants of the new housing estate. Apart from a stroll through the grounds of Braunstone Hall, which became a public park, there was little else in the way of entertainment. The Roxy served the community for 35 years before closing in 1968. The building was reopened as a bingo hall for some years but has now been demolished after a major fire which ravaged the building on the night of 12 December 2002. Another serious fire occurred in Braunstone on 1 March 1966, when a huge blaze raged through the living accommodation of the Blessed Sacrament Fathers, in Braunstone Avenue. The *Leicester Mercury* of 2 March 1966 reported that: '... flames could be seen half a mile away on Hinckley Road.' The church of the Blessed Sacrament, with its distinctive copper roof, was built in 1954.

The very small area known as Braunstone Frith is sandwiched between Western Park and the Corporation Golf Course, together with Oakmeadow Spinney. Apart from its very small population and the Braunstone Frith Junior and Infant School there would be little to say about the area, had the redoubtable John Throsby not paid a visit in 1790. In his travels around the area he wrote: '... then taking the crossroads you pass over a part of

Cottages on the former Winstanley Estate in 1973.

Leicester Forest. The first place of any consequence is a little sheltered moated dwelling, called Frith Hall, occupied by Mr Woodland, a Quaker, a man of extensive fortune, a scholar, and a humourist when in humour.' It might be wondered whether Mr Woodland found some humour in his own name, living so close to the forest! The hall appears on Carey's map of 1819 as Frith Hall and on a 1960s map as Kirby Frith Hall. It disappears on later maps. The golf course and spinney are still there.

Wartime hospital huts.

Braunstone Hall Primary School, set in delightful gardens. Until the 1920s it was home to the Winstanley family for several generations.

Further reading:

Leicester City Council, *A Short History of Braunstone Park*, Leicester City Council, undated.

Wilshere, J., *Old Braunstone*, 2nd edition, Leicester Research Department of Chamberlain Music and Books, 1984.

The Winstanley Manuscripts, DG5, unpublished

Clarendon Park

A large house with its surrounding estate once owned by John Biggs, close to Leicester Race Course, now Victoria Park, was demolished in 1863 and was the beginning of what was to become the area known as Clarendon Park. In 1867 Knighton Park Road was laid out in the spacious grounds which had formed part of the Biggs estate. The layout for the new area incorporated a long narrow lane, which led to four racecourses. The corners of two of these just reached to Victoria Park Road, opposite what was then Leicester Racecourse. The lane became known as Dukes Drive and continued to be used for horse riding for a number of years after the area had become built up. The name Dukes Drive was probably intended to emulate that of Rotten Row in London, the rather superior name leaving no doubt about the superiority of its users. Within three years a number of substantial properties had been completed. A plan of 1877 shows that a considerable part of the area that was to become Clarendon Park consisted mainly of fields. The largest plot, at more than 29 acres, was Spinney Close, which reached from the toll house on Welford Road to roughly where Gainsborough Road is today. To the east of Welford Road it stretched to what is now Lorne Road. The fields had such names as Big Holmes, Little Holmes, Big Three Corners, Cow Close and Clover Close. A sizeable amount of land was bought by Alfred Donisthorpe, Charles Smith and Samuel Francis Stone, who set up the Clarendon Park Company. Three of the roads were named after Francis Stone's sons

Ormidale on Knighton Park Road, in 1914. It was the home of chemist and dentist, George Woolley, JP; his business address was at 48, London Road.

Knighton Park Road in the process of demolition.

Cecil, Howard and Montague, the former being changed to Cecilia Road when it was realised that a Cecil Road already existed, not far away in the Highfields area. In 1889 the land was sold to Samuel Davis, who had West, Central and East Avenues drawn up. The cheapest local tender for the job was submitted by Holland's, at £6,198 16s 5d. Samuel Stone had lived at the Woodlands, which gave its name to Woodland Avenue, laid out in the grounds of Stoneygate House.

R.G. Waddington, writing in the *Leicester Mercury* on 25 April 1931, recalled a conversation with W.J. Freer, the Clerk to the County Council. Freer's grandfather could remember in his youth a magnificent row of elm trees that reached from the common land close to Pocklingtons Walk, all the way to Oadby, a distance of some five miles. It is thought that the trees were planted early in the 18th century. In 1931 it was still possible to locate the position of the trees as some had been retained in East and West Avenues and others were to be found in the gardens of Stoneygate's grand houses. It is also likely to be the reason why Elms Road was thus named.

The solidly Victorian densely packed red-brick suburb was built mainly between 1875

The old almshouses in Clarendon Park Road, in 1965.

and 1890, when the Clarendon Park Estate was divided into building plots and sold. There were initially 13 small estates in the area but the names of these seem only to have been used early on. The Springfield Estate was one of these; the road of the same name still possesses a number of large houses. In May 1889, land in Springfield Road sold for 12s 2d a square yard. The site of Springfield House, from which the estate took its name, is now occupied by Clarendon Park Congregational Church. The church was designed by Leicester architect James Tait (1835–1915) and built in 1885–6 of Mountsorrel granite. It was another Leicester architect of note, Isaac Barradale (1845–1892), who purchased some of the land in the area and designed a number of houses, with an eye to speculative sales. Leicester's most well-known national architect and designer, Ernest Gimson (1864–1919), was articled to Barradale in the 1880s. In 1897, Gimson designed the White House on North Avenue for Arthur Gimson. The substantial house is limewashed, with a Swithland slate roof. The interior has plasterwork friezes also designed by Ernest Gimson. The house was later occupied by Harold Gimson, a director of Gimson and Co. (Leicester) Ltd, ironfounders and engineers, whose premises were on Vulcan Road.

In the early part of the 20th century, another familiar Leicester name, Francis Young, lived at No.11 North Avenue. He was the son of Joseph Young, whose pharmacy and photographic business was in Gallowtree Gate for many years.

The area, particularly towards the Welford Road, was largely one of speculatively built terraced housing. Although it has been suggested that the suburb was considered to be lower middle class, there were many substantial three-storey villas. On the main roads these had attic rooms for maids and gardens to the front and rear.

Clarendon Park Road and Queens Road were busy shopping areas, as they still are today. No.66 Queens Road was a hairdressers that doubled as the Midland Railway Receiving Office. Coincidentally No.66 Clarendon Park Road was a firm of painters that doubled as a registry office. On the same road is Clarendon Park Methodist Church, a large building with Gothic elements and an octagonal tower, designed in 1900 by Albert Edwin Sawday (1851–1923). The Sawdays were yet another notable firm of Leicester architects, with further generations practising throughout the 20th century until the present day. Albert Sawday, in his practice with Francis Redfern, had also designed a number of houses in the area, including his own, at No.14 Springfield Road.

Until recently there were allotments off the south end of Queens Road, an oasis behind the bustle of shops and traffic. These have sadly been replaced with housing. Allotments were a major feature of working and lower middle class suburban life, but regrettably few remain.

The rather magnificent St John the Baptist Church of England was designed by Goddard and Paget in 1884–5. The Infants and Junior School opened in 1890. The municipal library on Clarendon Park Road, known as Knighton Library, was opened in 1895. In the early years of the 20th century it opened on weekdays from 6.30am to 10pm and on Saturdays from 3pm to 10pm. No doubt the poor librarians needed the Saturday morning to do their shopping, particularly as many shops in the town would close on a Saturday afternoon. The combined Police and Fire Engine Station was situated on Queens Road until the beginning of World War One, when the Fire Service ceased its operations there; the Police Station remained until 1929. In 1892 Knighton Public Hall, on Clarendon Park Road, opened to serve the sizeable suburb. In 1913 plans to convert it to a cinema were drawn up by Wakerley and Wells and it opened in the same year. The building itself is worthy of note, with a red-brick and stone-banded triangular façade, and some interesting carving in the stonework. The nearby residents were somewhat apprehensive about a cinema on their doorstep and the company, determined to make the operation a success, held a private matinee for those living in the area on 13 February 1913. The cinema, with a seating capacity of about 500, opened as the Lyric but within a few months had changed its name to the Knighton. The venture was not altogether a success, as it closed after only three years, in 1916.

Clarendon Park is now a lively and popular middle-class area, with many residents having links with the University of Leicester. It also has a touch of suburban London, with its two major commercial roads having a wide variety of specialist shops and restaurants.

Further reading:

Boynton, H. and D. Seaton, *From Tollgate to Tramshed The History of London Road Leicester c.1860–1920*, published by the authors, 1999.

Gill, R., *Walks Through Victorian Leicester*, The Leicester Victorian Society, 1994.

Thornton, P., *Clarendon Park*, published by the author, 1990.

Williams, D. R., *Cinema in Leicester 1896–1931*, Heart of Albion Press, 1993.

Crown Hills

The ridge of land known as Crown Hills could be reached by a very early trackway from Tilton. In prehistoric times a view of the land that would eventually become the city of Leicester would have been clearly visible from here. It was previously part of Evington, which consisted of three agricultural estates. The central estate, which was to be developed as Crown Hills, was in the possession of a lifelong tenant, the Reverend F.G. Burnaby. Revd Burnaby had already begun to develop parts of North Evington in the 1870s. Crown Hills was transferred to the borough of Leicester in 1892 and in 1896 it became part of Leicester civil parish. It is perhaps best known for its association with the architect, Arthur Wakerley (1862–1931), who developed much of North Evington. Wakerley had been a youthful mayor of Leicester, 1897–8, being elected at the age of 35. Wakerley had become familiar with the area as the assistant of the architect James Bird Snr, who was surveyor to the Billesdon Rural Sanitary Board, under whose jurisdiction the land came. Wakerley saw the potential for further development. Arthur Wakerley was a devout Methodist and philanthropist who wanted to provide pleasant suburban housing for the workers, in close proximity to the factories in which they would be employed. He also provided a market hall and many other amenities but sadly for many, as a teetotaller he provided no public house!

Wakerley offered favourable rates to tempt commercial enterprise to establish itself two miles from the city centre, which was not an easy task as good public transport was not yet available in the area. His first purchase of land in the area was in 1885 and Gwendolen Road was the first to be developed in 1887. The road was named after his first child, who had been born that year. Other roads were named after those who were associated with the development of the area, including the Reverend Burnaby and Sir John Rolleston, his agent. Orson Street was named after the Conservative builder and land agent Orson Wright, a man who had a hand in the development of a number of the new areas of the expanding town The new suburb was separated from Evington village by a great swathe of open countryside, not to be built upon until the 1950s, when the Goodwood Estate was built.

Wakerley gave a substantial amount of land to the Wycliffe Society for Helping the Blind in 1897. A hall of residence and six cottage homes were designed by Wakerley and opened by his wife Bertha in 1906. The Society obtained a further plot of land from Wakerley at a very favourable rate and six villas were constructed in around 1915. A Work Institute was added in the 1920s. In addition to the fine buildings one of the most charming features in Gwendolen Road is Gwendolen Gardens, or perhaps 'secret gardens' would be more appropriate, as the discreet entrance is scarcely discernible from the road.

Highcross House, Gwendolen Road, the house Arthur Wakerley designed for his daughter Gwendolen and her husband Leslie. The house was a reconstruction of one that had stood in Highcross Street and the pillar was the last remaining one from the High Cross in Leicester.

Green Lane Close, with one of Arthur Wakerley's £299 houses.

The gardens were originally planted with many fragrantly perfumed plants for the residents of the hall and cottage homes to enjoy. The gardens are still appreciated by local residents today, as they provide a pleasant, quiet oasis in a built-up area.

Much of the land in the area was owned by the Leicester Freehold Land Society, which Arthur Wakerley had instigated. The land was thus owned by a relatively large number of people, rather than one extremely wealthy landowner. Although there were wealthy members of the society, including manufacturers like Samuel Faire of Faire Brothers and numerous architects and builders, there were also those of more modest means who lived in similar areas to those they were investing their money in. There were also, perhaps surprisingly for the Victorian period, quite a number of women members of the society. Other eminent architects were involved in streets bordering Crown Hills, such as Joseph Goddard and Isaac Barradale. When the streets were first laid out, they delighted in such charming names as the Burnaby Park Estate.

Wakerley's enthusiasm for the area was eventually to extend to him designing a house for himself at Crown Hills, as well as residences for other members of his family. He moved into Crown Hill House, situated near the top of the hill on Gwendolen Road in 1915 (not to be confused with Crown Hills House further down the road, which was a dairy). There was also an estate farm, managed by Wakerley's son-in-law. The Aberdeen Angus cows that had arrived by train from Scotland were driven along the roads from the station to the farm, something that would still have been a familiar sight even into the 1920s. Wakerley made himself popular with the local children at harvest time when they were allowed to play in the fields and he would throw apples to them. In 1923 Highcross House was erected for his eldest daughter in the grounds of Crown Hill House. It was a reconstruction of a house that had stood in Highcross Street and was due to be demolished. Wakerley bought the bricks and timber and had the house rebuilt. He had a great interest in antiquities and in 1919 had acquired the remaining pillar of the Highcross and had it erected in the garden of Crown Hill. Mrs Wakerley had expressed a wish that after her death it should be returned to the city and it now resides in Cheapside. The Hor-Stone from Evington, similar to the Humber Stone, was also obtained by Wakerley and displayed in the garden of Highcross

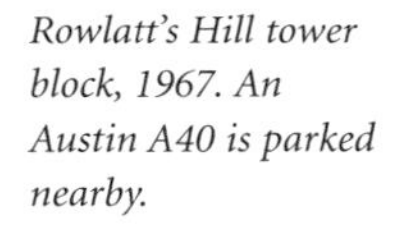

Rowlatt's Hill tower block, 1967. An Austin A40 is parked nearby.

The stark tower blocks in Rowlatt's Hill contrasting with the spacious gardens below.

House. In 1920 Wakerley completed a pair of semi-detached houses for his sister and his gardener. These reflected work he had been doing on a £299 council house, but used superior quality materials.

Wakerley's semi-detached £299 house was an innovative solution to the tremendous housing shortage after World War One. Many local authorities had been seeking a relatively cheap and rapid answer to the problem. Wakerley's initial design, produced in 1922, cost £450 but was rejected. Undeterred Wakerley went back to his drawing board and produced the design familiar to many local people for £299. The first 18 houses were constructed later that year in Crown Hills, in Green Lane Close, while many others were built in other areas of Leicester, some of which are now listed buildings.

Perhaps the most familiar building near to Crown Hills is the General Hospital. It was built on a 62-acre site in 1905, originally as the Leicester or North Evington Poor Law Institution, and it had space for 512 patients. During World War One it was used for wounded soldiers and was renamed the North Evington War Hospital. The many visitors would alight at the tram stop at the bottom of Gwendolen Road. The hospital was returned to the Poor Law Guardians in the summer of 1919 and in 1930 came under the management of the City Health Committee.

Crown Hills, or North Evington, or indeed 'New Evington' as it was known initially, is still a thriving suburb, with housing and industry operating side by side.

Further Reading:

Beazley, B., *Four Years Remembered: Leicester During the Great War*, The Breedon Books Publishing Company Limited, 1999.

Farquhar, J., *Arthur Wakerley, 1862–1931*, Sedgebrook Press, 1984.

EVINGTON

The centre of the old parish of Evington is about two and a half miles from Leicester's city centre. The village is of Anglo-Saxon origin and was previously known as Aefa's Tun and then Avintone. In the Domesday Book of 1086 the main landholder in the small village of Evington was Hugh de Grentemesnil, who held 10½ caracutes of land, the equivalent of over 2,000 acres, which he rented to a man called Ivo. Robert de Buci held the other caracute from the king. The village also had a mill and a meadow of 20 acres. A deer park was held by the lord of the manor and during the 14th century deer were stolen on two occasions. The village is near to the old Gartree Roman road and part of the parish was in the Gartree hundred.

The land was held for some time in the 13th century by Simon de Montfort, then for the next two centuries it was held by Sir Richard de Grey and his descendants. The dukes of Devonshire, who held it from about 1616 to 1734, were among a string of subsequent owners. Leicestershire historian John Throsby, writing in 1790, suggests that the last duke to own it probably lost it 'at cards or dice'. It was then purchased by Dr James Sherrard, who was born in Thurnby; in his will he bequeathed the manor to his five nieces and their families. An Act of Parliament was required before this could be carried out as it was not until the Married Women's Property Act was passed in 1882 that married women could own property, even if was left to them. By World War One Thomas Powys Keck

Granby Hill School, Evington Lane, in the 1860s.

Main Street on a postcard sent from Billesdon to Evington in 1906. The sender writes: 'will drive if time'. Motoring in the 1900s was still a hazardous affair, even over a few miles, and horse-drawn transport was less inclined to break down.

Coronation day in Evington in 1911. Both sexes are sporting a wonderful array of hats.

owned much of the village, but not long after the war ended he sold his estate, the main buyer being the Co-operative Wholesale Society. Part of the parish to the north transferred to Leicester County Borough in 1892 and in 1896 it merged with Leicester civil parish. Prior to this Evington had been a fairly small rural village, showing little increase in the population until the 1870s. In the 1920s there was still a vestige of a footpath from Evington to Leicester, which began on the other side of a stile at the end of Evington Road. In 1936 most of Evington merged with Leicester, with two smaller areas becoming part of Oadby and Stoughton.

Evington remained very much an agricultural village, with much of the land used for grazing until the late 19th century. In 1881 its small population of 450 were mainly farm workers. There had been a few stockingers and framework knitters in the 18th century but these had never reached any great number. The northern part of the parish was developed from 1885. Much of the development of North Evington was the work of Arthur Wakerley, architect and Liberal councillor for the Borough of Leicester. The many new houses and factories springing up offered alternative employment and artisans outnumbered farm workers at the close of the 19th century.

The church of St Denis is of late 13th and early 14th century origin. In 1867 the prestigious Leicester architectural practice of Henry Goddard and Son designed the chancel and organ chamber. Restoration work was carried out in 1884 by the same firm, which had become Goddard and Paget. Evington vicarage was rebuilt at a cost of £598 10s in 1839, to the designs of William Parsons (1797–1857) who had also designed the immense castellated fortress of Leicester Gaol in 1828. The vicarage was unfortunately demolished in the late 1970s, while the gaol is still very much in use! To the west of the church is Piggy's Hollow, the site of the old moated manor house, where there were also several fishponds and a water mill. Nicholas Pevsner writes that the site is 'one of the best in the county'. The church stands on tree-lined Shady Lane. Renowned over the decades for its popularity with courting couples, it still retains a certain picture postcard charm. At the other end of the lane is the Leicester Arboretum, opened in 1970, on 54 acres of

Evington village, 1904. The car is a very early model, c.1898–1904.

Shady Lane, c.1900.

land on the corner of Shady Lane and Stoughton Road. Evington can still boast a village green, with two 18th-century thatched cottages, and there are also some attractive 19th-century houses and cottages, although some recent rebuilding has taken place. Until the advent of the Evington horse bus service, the carriers cart, operated in 1828 by William Grant, left from the Wellington and Castle in Granby Street every Saturday. The Baptist Chapel on Main Street is also close to the village green. It was built in 1837, the cost being met by Samuel Davenport of Leicester, who also paid the minister's salary. The chapel

The height of summer in around 1900. Ladies with a pram and a horse-drawn van are in the background.

The Baptist Chapel and Manse, c.1900.

was designed in the fashionable but, for a nonconformist place of worship, highly unusual Gothic style. This perhaps owes something to the fact that the Baptists formed a breakaway movement from the parish church but continued to use a similar form of worship. The movement was known as the Countess of Huntingdon's Connexion. The small, stuccoed and pinnacled building is a gem, remaining in use and virtually unchanged since it was built. An organ, once owned by Queen Victoria and Price Albert, was later purchased for the chapel. The barge-boarded manse of the same period was sadly demolished as a result of a road-widening scheme and replaced with a plainer building in 1964. In 1895 the Primitive Methodist Chapel in Leicester Street was built, primarily to serve the new suburb of North Evington. On Main Street, the building that has been the Cedars Hotel since 1937 was once the home of the prolific novelist and short story writer, E. Phillips Oppenheim.

The Italianate Evington Hall in Spencefield Lane was built for Henry Coleman in the 1840s, although he had purchased the land many years earlier in 1816. The hall was later purchased by John Edward Faire, who with his brother Sir Samuel Faire, JP, was joint managing director of Faire Brothers and Co. They owned several factories in Leicester, and the largest and most ornate still survives in Rutland Street. The firm made a variety of haberdashery goods for the thriving boot and shoe trade, including the 'electric lace'! The *Leicester Mercury* of 6 September 1982, in an interview with the widow of John Faire's chauffeur, recalls the decade after the World War One, when the family owned

A postcard sent to Skegness in August 1906. The sender writes that they have had 'a most enjoyable holiday'.

three cars – a 'gleaming Rolls Royce' being used exclusively by Mr Faire. At the other end of the social spectrum, the widow remembered that visiting Leicester herself involved at least a two-mile walk to the tram stop on Evington Road. Often she would walk all the way to the city centre, with her two young children in a pram. John Faire died in 1929

Evington horse bus or charabanc, at the end of the 19th or beginning of the 20th century.

and the house was apparently empty for some years, until it was used in the 1930s for refugee children fleeing from the Basque country during the Spanish Civil War. The hall became Evington Convent School in 1940 and is now St Paul's Roman Catholic School.

Evington House was built by Colonel John Burnaby in 1836. He was the third son of Anna Burnaby, who was a great niece of Dr Sherrard and inherited the Evington land through her mother Mary. John Burnaby and his wife Anne had 11 children, and they moved with their two unmarried daughters to Evington House after his retirement from the Grenadier Guards. He died in 1852. His daughters continued to live in the house until they died in the 1880s. The house was let to a number of people until the Burnaby family sold it to John Dearden in 1902. During World War One it was used as an auxiliary hospital, and in 1919 Mr and Mrs Frank Pochin purchased the house for £6,000. The house was sold again in 1931 to Leicester architect Tom Trevor Sawday and his wife Dorothy, the daughter of Arthur Wakerley. The house became the headquarters of the Evington Home Guard Platoon during World War Two, with the Sawdays still in residence. The house suffered some bomb damage during the war, including a hole in the roof made by two unexploded bombs.

In 1947 the house and sur-

Old cottages, 1904.

Shady Lane, 1900.

rounding 44-acre estate were purchased for use as a public park, which opened on a delightfully sunny day during the Whitsuntide holiday of 1948. The *Leicester Mercury* of 4 October 1949, reported with enthusiasm on the new park: 'The lawns and playing fields are, for Leicester, quite a thing of their own. They are graciously adorned with trees, evergreen and deciduous…'. The house was a focal point of the park, with a café and changing rooms for those using the sports facilities. Like many suburban parks the pavilion café is a thing of the past but the park itself, with panoramic views over Leicester, still remains popular with local residents.

Evington National School opened in 1841, funded by John Burnaby. In 1935 it became part of Leicester Education Committee and was demolished in 1964. In the same year the Boys Club, which had used the old school building, had a new building opened in Evington by the singer Frankie Vaughan, who was an ardent supporter of the Boys Club movement.

North Evington horse bus, c.1890.

The village hall, or the King George V Memorial Hall, was built in 1912 to celebrate the King's coronation. The village hall was obviously a valuable amenity for the village, which was now a part of the expanding suburb, and on 16 October 1916 the Evington Cinema was to add another dimension to entertainment. Despite the name, however, the Evington Cinema was

Main Street and Spencefield Lane in 1921.

Shady Lane with a solitary car in the 1950s.

situated on East Park Road in North Evington, some distance from the village but close to the relatively new suburban area that had grown to the west of the old village of Evington. Admission was free to the opening celebrations of the new cinema, and a ladies' orchestra, a café and patrons' lounge were there to entice the prospective cinema-goer. The opening film, poignantly but appropriately, in view of the wartime situation,

Evington in the 1930s.

was *Spirit of France*, starring Jane Hading. The posters announced: 'A Great Cinematic Production of a Thrilling War Story'. In 1916, halfway through World War One, a cinema ticket was 2d, 4d, or 6d downstairs and 9d in the balcony, plus War Tax. The Evington closed as a cinema in April 1979. The *Leicester Mercury* of 25 September 1979 reported on the cinema's closure. Although the cinema no longer exists, the magnificent building is still in use and the rear has been converted to flats.

During World War Two, on 10 April 1941, a very unfortunate incident occurred in Evington when an English pilot, in an attempt to impress his girlfriend who lived on St Denys Road, flew his five-crew bomber at rooftop-skimming height. The resulting serious accident with a chimney sadly killed the lady occupant of the house who was in her garden at the time.

Development in the village had happened gradually after it was incorporated into the borough of Leicester, but it grew apace in the 1930s. In 1951, the Mayflower Primary School opened on Evington Drive to serve the expanding suburb. In 1954 the Evington Homes for Aged Pilgrims was opened, the charitable society having been formed in London in 1808 to assist elderly practising Christians.

In 1989 Evington village was declared a conservation area.

Further reading:
Leicester City Council, *A Short History of Evington Park*, undated.

Evington before World War Two. Teas and Hovis are advertised at the local shop, while the Baptist Chapel and Manse can be seen in the background.

Very old thatched cottages, photographed in 1921.

Evington village, c.1900.

John Bull Tyres, Evington Valley Road, in the 1930s. The car on the left is a late 1920s Morris Cowley, the others are early 1930s.

Shady Lane, looking even more picturesque in the snow, c.1895.

A lovely sunny day for the opening of Evington Park in May 1948.

The exquisite Baptist Chapel in 1960, situated on the corner of Main Street and High Street. The equally charming manse to the left was unfortunately demolished in a road-widening scheme.

Eyres Monsell

The area known as Eyres Monsell was previously part of the estate of Samuel Eyres (born 1796) of Armley, Yorkshire. His estates then passed to Henry William Eyres, who lived at Dumbleton Hall, in the village of Dumbleton, Worcestershire. The property had been acquired by the Eyres family in 1875. Henry's daughter Caroline Mary Sybil Eyres, Viscountess Monsell, was born on 21 August 1881. In 1904 she married Bolton Meredith Monsell, who took the name of Eyres on his marriage, changing the family name to Eyres-Monsell. Bolton Eyres-Monsell was a Conservative whip in 1911 and was chief Conservative whip from 1923 to 1931. He was also the Member of Parliament for Evesham and from 1930 to 1935 First Lord of the Admiralty. On 30 November 1935 he was created 1st Viscount Monsell of Evesham.

Left and below: The now busy Saffron Lane roundabout in 1953, with a view across to the new Eyres Monsell Estate.

Children on the Eyres Monsell Estate in 1956.

Eyres Monsell shopping centre, 1956.

The Eyres-Monsells continued in ownership of their Leicestershire estates until they were compulsorily purchased from the Rt Hon. Viscountess Monsell, CBE, who held the land in her own right, by the Corporation of Leicester in 1950–51. The first purchase of land consisted of 243,221 acres for £25,000; £15,500 secured the second lot, consisting of 131,268 acres. The Eyres Monsell Estate was to become the second largest estate in

The new school being prepared in 1953.

Leicester built after World War Two. The area was rural and the land had been previously used for agricultural purposes. The area today is redolent of a country estate, although there was never a grand house at the centre of it. There are wide green spaces with mature trees, something not always apparent in local authority housing areas.

The Corporation's Development Plan for Leicester provided for almost every need of the future inhabitants of the proposed housing estate of Eyres Monsell. One small difficulty, which was overcome, was that the Corporation also needed land in the county. Proposals for the Eyres Monsell Estate were a vast improvement on the high-rise blocks of flats built by many local authorities to solve the housing crisis in the aftermath of World War Two. Four hundred 'Easiform' houses, constructed from pre-cast concrete sections, were initially planned in 1951 and built by John Laing and Son Ltd. A report in the *Illustrated Leicester Chronicle*, 9 May 1953, on the rapid expansion of the city notes that: 'Another vast city and county estate is under construction at Eyres Monsell, south Leicester. There are nearly seven hundred homes occupied there up to date.' A further 1,300 were projected. The council tried to avoid the uniformity that often arose with mass housing, by interspersing brick with concrete and using brightly coloured roof tiles and different shades of rendering. The plans allowed for doctors, midwives, policemen, schools and shops, together with a new Church of England. The firm of Basil Spence and

Sturdee Road, 1982.

A smart house in Eyres Monsell, 30 years on in 1982.

Partners, which had designed the new Coventry Cathedral and the church of St Aidan on the New Parks Estate, was chosen for this task. Unfortunately Spence's plan for the church, St Hugh's on Sturdee Road, was not carried out. Only the hall, which opened in 1958, was ever built, and it served as the church. The plans for the vicarage that Spence had designed also remained on the drawing board.

Viscount Monsell died at the age of 88 in 1969 but not only does the name of Eyres Monsell live on in the name of the estate, the naval connection is also maintained in the names of the roads. Many of these recall former admirals and captains, such as Tovey, Bentinghouse and Sturdee. Sir Frederick Sturdee (1859–1925) was a World War One naval commander who was made Admiral of the Fleet in 1921. In his retirement he was largely responsible for the restoration of Nelson's flagship, *Victory*.

The smaller suburb or village of Glen Parva is south of Eyres Monsell; the area is divided between the city and the county, with the larger residential area being in the city. The village could once boast a moated building and pottery from the Middle Ages was found when the moat was excavated. A chapel of ease to Aylestone is thought to have existed there in the early 13th century. The part outside the city boundary consisted largely of the local barracks and a brickworks, which ceased operating only a few years ago.

Further reading:
The Dustsheet, No.22, Autumn 2002.
Bonney, M., *Eyres Monsell*, Leicester.

Nearly finished: the Eyres Monsell Junior School in 1955.

Humberstone

Humberstone is situated two and a half miles north-east of Leicester. In 1086 Hugh de Grentemesnil held the manor of Humberstone, which included 12 acres of meadow and nine caracutes of land (roughly 900 acres). By around 1130 it is thought that the land had passed to the earls of Leicester, although there were three other landowners at this time, Roger de Ramis, Walter de Musters and Ralph de Martival. The de Martivals were connected with Humberstone until the middle of the 14th century. The Martival name is still in use as one of the roads on the Tailby Estate in New Humberstone. From 1519 to 1614 the Keble family held the land. Their lands were confiscated for a time because Jane, the wife of Henry Keble, was a recusant, someone who refused to attend Church of England services, either Catholic or Protestant. The land may have been taken in lieu of the fine of one shilling a week for not attending. In 1581 this was raised to £20 a month, a vast sum in the 16th century. It could be profitable for the Church of England to re-invoke the law today! The views of the Hastings family, who were the next owners, were also met with disapproval by the establishment, and they were heavily fined by Parliament for their support of Charles I. Thomas Sutton of London was the next owner and in 1755 his son sold the manors to William Pochin, MP, of Barkby Hall. The Pochin family are still very much associated with the village of Barkby.

A church is first mentioned in Humberstone in the 13th century, and a little of the mediaeval church still remains, namely the tower and part of the chancel outer walls. Most of the church of St Mary was rebuilt in 1857–58 to the designs of Raphael Brandon. Brandon also worked on the church of St Martin, which became Leicester Cathedral in

Humberstone Drive.

Cottages at the junction of Thurmaston Lane and Gipsy Lane, demolished in 1939.

1927. He used the local Humberstone alabaster for the interior and produced an unusual but delightful combination of an alabaster frieze with terracotta flowers above the stalls.

The centre of Humbertone still retains a number of very pleasing buildings spanning several hundred years of architectural history. Humberstone Manor in the Main Street is thought to be mostly 17th century, although there is some older brickwork. It was extended at the end of the 18th century and has a date of 1789 on the gable. The house and 400-year-old tithe barn became part of the Towers Hospital complex, and the barn was later remodelled for use as living accommodation. Close to Humberstone Manor is the site of the mediaeval fishponds. The Manor House, also on Main Street, is of 18th-century origin, having three storeys and chequered brickwork. Monks Rest, on Vicarage Lane, is a three-storey stuccoed house built in the first half of the 19th century. There was also the rather delightful Humberstone Hall, late 18th or early 19th century, with intricate ironwork and an orangery, now demolished. The hall was reached via an

St Mary's Church, 1904.

The Towers Hospital model farm, built in 1936 at a cost of £18,000.

impressive avenue of Wellingtonias, which later became Pine Tree Avenue. Halfway along the driveway to the hall was the 'The Paddocks', a dwelling whose tenant was the hall bailiff in the 19th century.

Humberstone had always been quite a sizeable village and from the early 18th century the population increased considerably, as it became a centre for framework knitting. Suburbanisation encroached on Humberstone as the village and the town of Leicester gradually expanded. In 1821 the population of Humberstone was 415, having hardly changed over the centuries, but in the next 40 years it would more than double.

In 1830 Humberstone was part of the chapelry of Goscote. There were 1,225 acres of land and 103 houses, with 415 inhabitants. The inhabitants in the 1830s had three public houses to sit and quaff their ale in. The downside was that the 500-year-old Old Plough

The exterior of the tithe barn (left) . The interior of the 17th-century tithe barn in Humberstone.

Inn also contained the village lock-up! Drunks would be detained overnight, before being thrown out in a rather more sober state the next morning. The Plough was demolished in 1963 and the *Leicester Mercury* of 29 November 1963 interviewed the regulars, some of whom had been customers for over 70 years. They recalled that one room was used for sittings of the magistrate's court, that the highwayman Dick Turpin had lodged in the inn and that the cellar contained the best beer in Leicester. A new Swedish-style pub was soon built on the site but the regulars must surely have missed the cosiness of the Old Plough. Until the mid-19th century Humberstone, like many large villages, had been relatively self-sufficient: it could boast, among other trades, a miller and cabinetmaker, and in 1895 there were still a maltster or brewer, a carpenter, blacksmith and bootmaker.

The Humber Stone, an ignominious piece of rock that is said to have all kinds of magic powers.

New Humberstone begins to appear in the parish registers of 1880 and was the part of the parish nearest the boundary with the borough of Leicester. A number of Leicester tradespeople had their substantial villas built on Victoria Road East, Overton Road and Uppingham Road. A wide variety of commercial enterprises were already established on these roads in the late 19th century. In 1914 among the butchers and sweet shops or the 'hard confectioners', as they were known, were also the makers of artificial teeth, a number of market gardens and a branch of the Leicester Public Medical Service. The main commercial area of the Uppingham Road has several interesting buildings, including the Leicester Co-operative Society's store, designed in a magnificent Arts and Crafts style.

In 1892, with the extension of the Leicester borough boundaries, a quarter of Humberstone became part of Leicester. The borough had hoped to gain all of Humberstone parish, but it had to be content until 1935, when almost the whole of Humberstone became part of what had by then become the city of Leicester.

In a letter to the *Leicester Mercury* of 14 October 1950, a reader recalls his boyhood days in New Humberstone. He attended the Newby Street Congregational Church Sunday School in the 1880s. Sunday School outings were often to Ingarsby, travelling by train on the Great Northern Line from Humberstone Station. The excursions would have been occasions of great excitement and were probably the highlight of the year for many

The faded Regency splendour of Humberstone Hall, with its circular garden house.

children, being the only time they would have travelled by train. The *Mercury* correspondent fared better than many children of the day, travelling by train from Humberstone to Belgrave Road Station on visits to the Abbey Park in the holidays, the fare being 1d or 1½d.

The name Humberstone is thought to derive from 'Hunbeorht's Stone', and Humberstone does indeed possess a stone, which is of Mountsorrel granite and possibly of Celtic origin. Writing in the 1920s local historian S.H. Skillington referred to it as a monolith called the Host Stone, and notes that it 'is also said to have been the resort of fairies, and to have exercised a malign influence upon parishioners who treated it with disrespect.' The stone is also known as the 'Humber' and the 'Hell Stone' and countless other variations. It is situated near Thurmaston Lane and Sandhills Avenue and has aroused much superstition and speculation over the centuries. Other stories suggest that in 1750 the curate who owned the land on which the stone stood attempted to bury it so that the land could be more easily ploughed. Shortly after this had been accomplished he was thrown from his gig and killed. Early in the 19th century the next owner of the field, irritated by the presence of the stone, attempted to break it into pieces and succeeded in knocking a piece off. Six years later in 1810 he too met with considerable misfortune: having been the farmer of a substantial acreage he died in poverty in the workhouse. In 1878 William Pochin of Barkby was said to have accidentally shot off half of his hand after investigating the stone. Another tale tells of a man who was said to have heard the

The conveniently placed footpath between St Mary's church and the Windmill Inn, 1956.

stone emitting groaning noises, who fled in terror. Whether he had partaken of a quantity of ale beforehand is not recorded! In the 18th century the historian John Nichols wrote that there was a cell, or very small monastery, in Humberstone, where six brothers or friars lived. It was said that if a brother travelling between Leicester Abbey and Launde

New Humberstone: St Barnabas' Library, French Road, in 1937. It was designed by Symington, Prince and Pike.

should arrive at the monastery at around 8am the brothers should provide him with breakfast and a pint of beer, if noon a dinner and beer, if eight at night, supper, lodging and breakfast. The building was demolished in around 1726. Nichols also notes rather wryly that there may have been another religious house or nunnery to the north-west of the village, close to the Humber Stone and that '… those who are fond of the marvellous have not failed to say, that there was a subterraneous passage from thence to Leicester Abbey.' Nichols obviously realised that a three-mile tunnel to what are now the ruins of the abbey on Abbey Park, was highly unlikely! The stone is now a listed monument and thus hopefully saved from human interference. As its weight may be 15–20 tons, any attempt to move it by magic or otherwise might present a considerable problem. Vandals, however, have sadly wrecked information boards and seating in the area.

As the suburb of Humberstone grew a park was opened in 1928 on 20 acres of land on the south side of Uppingham Road, opposite Humberstone Drive. Humberstone could also boast its own open-air swimming pool, the Leicester Lido, advertised as having 'half a million gallons of pure water'. This was situated in Scraptoft Lane, not far from the tram terminus. After its closure it became a trout farm, and the *Leicester Mercury* of 6 June 1975 reported: 'Tailpiece: Anglers are not allowed to dive in and swim after fish.' The Trocadero Cinema, at the apex of Uppingham Road and Scraptoft Lane, was another leisure venue for Humberstone. The cinema opened on 1 October 1931, showing *The Toast of Belgium* starring Dodo Watts. During the early 1930s, when Humberstone was outside the city boundary, the Trocadero was able to screen *Frankenstein*, which had been banned by the Leicester Watch Committee. By the time the *Leicester Mercury* of 11 and 12 September 1967 reported the destruction of the cinema in a major fire, it had already succumbed to the fate of many cinemas of the 1930s and become a bingo hall. Despite assertions that it would reopen, it became a petrol station.

Further reading:

Humberstone Village Community Forum, Three Circular Walks in and Around Humberstone, Leicestershire County Council, 2002.

Zientek, M. and J., *Humberstone Village and Church Through the Centuries*, published by the authors, 2000.

Humberstone Garden Suburb

The Garden City or Garden Suburb was a relatively new concept in design in the 1900s. Leicester was eventually to have several areas that were based on the ideas of the Garden City movement. The areas chosen were always well outside the town, to avoid the noise and pollution of the factories, and the houses were not densely packed like many of those on the edge of the town centre. The emphasis was on space and greenery, both in the roads, which usually curved, unlike the endless straight rows of 19th-century terraced housing, and in spacious gardens. Buildings that served the community, such as a church, school and other amenities, would be included in the plan. If the tenants and owners were fortunate enough there might also be a public house.

Humberstone Garden Suburb was built on 17 acres of land east of Humberstone village on Keyham Lane, and it included many of these features. The enterprising project was the work of the Anchor Boot and Shoe Productive Society, a co-operative manufacturing company, which was founded in 1893. The society was very successful and they were able to move from Causeway Lane to much better premises in Asfordby Street, North Evington. The factory had an education room where many illustrious visiting speakers came, including Ramsay Macdonald and Philip Snowdon. There were talks on a wide variety of subjects but two were particularly apt: 'The Garden City – A Solution to the Housing Problem' and 'Co-operation and the Housing of the People'. The workers were also inspired by a co-operative housing scheme established in Ealing and a talk given by Henry Vivian in 1902. From that year 45 of the workers began to save towards the project, and after looking at a number of sites they purchased the land in 1907, choosing a major architectural partnership, Barry Parker and Raymond Unwin, to design the layout. In 1903 Parker and Unwin had won a competition to design the first Garden City at Letchworth, Hertfordshire. Raymond Unwin went on to design the Shelthorpe Road Estate in Loughborough from 1926 until 1939. The architect George Hern designed many of the roughcast rendered houses between 1907 and 1911.

The estate was officially opened in October 1908 by Sir John and Lady Rolleston, after tenants had moved into the first two cottages. The houses were set in tree-lined roads, delighting in such names as Laburnham Road and Lilac Avenue. There were no more than 10 houses per acre, and they had large gardens for recreation and a degree of self-sufficiency. By 1915 there were 95 houses and 350 residents. The initial plan had been for 148 houses and the remaining 53 were eventually built. A church, meeting rooms, shops, a bowling green and tennis courts, plus a sizeable green space, created a communal village

Building Humberstone Garden Suburb.

atmosphere. Strangely, although the Garden Suburb was supplied with gas and water, electricity and mains sewerage were not included. The other major problem with the development was that despite its undoubtedly pleasant setting most of the tenants worked at the Anchor Factory on Asfordby Street. This was some two miles away in North Evington, close to Spinney Hill Park, where interestingly much of the area had been developed by Arthur Wakerley. However, tenants seemed to prefer the new Garden Suburb despite the distance, for although there was pleasant housing closer to the factories in the area, it could not compete with the attractive rural setting. Workers could take a tram from the Humberstone Road, although this was already over a mile away. One of the tenants, obviously fed up with this lengthy trek twice a day (including Saturdays!), and with 10 hours or so in the factory once there, started a bus service to the Corporation tram stop. Despite these few inconveniences, Humberstone Garden Suburb must have been infinitely better than living in the dense mass of housing closer to the town.

The small area is now almost submerged by three local authority housing estates. The newest, directly north, is the Hamilton Estate, built in the 1980s. To the east is the post-World War Two estate of Nether Hall. This takes its name from the Dower House to Scraptoft Hall. The house, just outside the city boundary in Scraptoft, was built for Sir Edmund Wigley in 1709. The Thurnby Lodge Estate to the south-east was also built after World War Two.

Further reading:

Nash, D. and Reeder, D., Eds, *Leicester in the Twentieth Century*, Alan Sutton in association with Leicester City Council, 1993.

Knighton

Knighton is situated two miles south-east of the city centre and although it was previously a chapelry of St Margaret's it was the only part of the parish outside the borough of Leicester. In 1892, 567 acres of Knighton were transferred to the borough. It had been argued that the remainder of the village was mainly agricultural and should not be included. In 1935 the remainder of the parish was included in the city of Leicester. Thus the old village of Knighton was to emerge in the 20th century as South and West Knighton.

The Poplars, Knighton, with its Swithland slate roof and immaculate flower beds. This was the former home of Alderman Billings, who was Lord Mayor 1933–34.

Records of Knighton first appear in the Domesday Book of 1086, which states that it was held by the Bishop of Lincoln and consisted of less than a hide of land. The population amounted to a mere 24. In 1143 the Earl of Leicester, Robert le Bossu, was granted land valued at £10 by Bishop Alexander. Le Bossu held it for one knight's fee and in 1218 it was returned to the see of Lincoln, remaining the property of the bishops until 1547, when Edward VI was granted the manor. Some 30 years later in 1577 Elizabeth I granted it to Matthew Farnham of Quorndon and Sir George Turpin of Knaptoft. Matthew Farnham left the manor to his son Humphrey. There are no records of who held the manor for the next 200 years. The property eventually passed to the Craddock family, who appear to have been in Leicester since at least the 1500s and although not listed as lords of the manor had been the major land owners since 1730, when the first Edmond Craddock, who was a woollen draper, bought land in Knighton. By 1800 Sir Edmond Craddock, a descendant, is recorded as being lord of the manor. He was the son of Mary Craddock and Joseph Bunney, and on the death of his maternal uncle he was left many properties in Knighton, at which point he took the name of Craddock. On his marriage to Anne Hurlock, the grand-daughter of Sir John Hartopp, he added the name Hartopp. The Craddocks continued their association with Knighton, and another Sir Edmond was lord of the manor in 1846. His descendant, yet another Sir Edmond, held the title in 1878 when he was also the principal of Brasenose College, Oxford. The Craddock family had literary and theatrical conections and Joseph Craddock, who spent his early life in Knighton and was probably born there in 1741, wrote at the age of 87 his *Literary and Miscellaneous Memoirs.* Another member of the family, born at the hall in 1814, was Charles Adderley, 1st Lord Norton. He achieved high political office as President of the Board of Trade in 1874, when Benjamin Disraeli was Prime Minister.

Knighton Road in the 1920s.

The Craddocks lived at the former manor house, Knighton Hall, parts of which date from the 17th century. The house was remodelled and extended in the early 1800s, to the designs of the Leicester architect John Johnson (1732–1814). In 1837 Sir Edmond Hartopp commissioned another local architect, Henry Goddard (1792–1868), to design a coach house and stables at the hall. Perhaps he was already thinking of ceasing to use the hall as his main residence, as in 1831 the hall was occupied by a Captain King. By 1846 the house was being used as a hunting lodge rather than a family home. Goddard also designed several cottages on Chapel Lane for Sir Edmond in 1838. Very few other buildings from the old village of Knighton survive, although the Craddock Arms, like the hall dating back to the 17th century, is fortunately still in business. On Church Lane north-east of the church in a setting of almost rural tranquility is the picturesque, thatched Oram Cottage, which like the other surviving buildings is likely to date from the 17th century. This was bequeathed to the city of Leicester in 1961 by Briseis Oram, the widow of Daniel Oram of Knighton Hall. Close by is the memorial porch to John Johnson of Knighton Fields, presented by his sister Mary after his death in 1877. The

Newmarket Street, 1900.

Chapel Lane in 1900. The chapel is partly hidden by trees.

timber and Mountsorrel granite porch serves as the churchyard entrance on Church Lane. The *Leicester Mercury* of 9 July 1969 carried a report on the demolition of the two oldest cottages in Knighton, which were thought to be nearly 500 years old. They had been owned by the Rodwell family, who had owned the local dairy for many years. When Knighton was enclosed in 1756 the land was divided between 17 families, three of these being Craddocks. Although there were a number of farming families, one of the other 14 to receive land was Edmond Johnson, a dyer. The village continued to expand and in 1831 there were 79 houses and 383 inhabitants. By 1832 only four of the landowners from the time of the enclosure remained. The Craddocks had sold much of their land prior to this date and a great deal more was disposed of for building in 1854. Colonel Edmond Craddock sold Knighton Hall to Leicester University in 1931, since when it has been used as the Vice-Chancellor's residence. The hall has a wonderful garden and arboretum.

Knighton was largely an agricultural village and in 1877 when the surrounding suburban areas of Clarendon Park and Stoneygate were becoming rapidly built up, Knighton still had three farms. In 1914 Tom Gould continued to farm at Knighton Farm on Church Road. During the 18th century a few trades were found in the village, including a stocking-weaver in 1712 and a carpenter and cordwainer or shoe-maker in 1756. In 1790 John Throsby mentions a Mr Hunt as being 'an eminent wool-stapler'. Mr Hunt lived on the estate of the Inge family, in 'a little open box', with a view of London Road in the distance. There was also framework knitting in the 18th century but this had declined by 1844. In the 1830s Knighton had the exclusivity that was to become its

Thatched cottages on Chapel Lane, photographed in 1894, shortly before they burnt down.

The meadow next to St Mary Magdalene Church in the 1900s.

Winter in Knighton in the 1890s. Chapel Lane: the house on the left was built in 1838.

trademark as a suburban area of high quality: there were no tradesmen in the village, no shops and no public house.

The parish church of St Mary Magdalene is of 13th and 14th century origin, with a soaring octagonal spire being added in the 15th century. High up in the east wall of the tower is a perpendicular statue of Mary Magdalene. Restoration work was carried out in 1860 and later in 1894 by national architect Ewan Christian, who designed and restored other Leicester churches. Knighton churchyard has a number of both sad and interesting epitaphs. Annie Elizabeth Greatorex, who was only a year old when she died in 1866, is buried there. Her names lives on in the cooking apple of the same name, produced by her father Samuel Greatorex. The apple won him a first-class certificate from the Royal Horticultural Society in 1868: no doubt always a poignant reminder of his little daughter. A memorial, in the shape of a tall stone cross, commemorates the death of Denzil J. Jarvis, who perished when the *Titanic* sank on 14 April 1912. He had been a former managing partner of the Leicester engineering company Wadkin's. The tiny church of St Guthlacs on Holbrook Road, with its delightful garden, was built as a chapel of ease to Knighton in 1912. The building, which was not completed, cost between £900 and £1,000 to build and was the last work of Stockdale Harrison, who died in 1914.

Suburbia began to creep up on the village from about 1880 with the development of New or South Knighton. South of Knighton Road a number of substantial houses had already been built before this date and a wide variety of housing had sprung up on Knighton Church Road and Knighton Road South.

A horse-drawn tram service began to operate from Leicester to Knighton Road from 1877, to serve the expanding area. In 1904 these trams were replaced by electric ones. In

Knighton Post Office and General Stores on the corner of Knighton Lane and Newmarket Street. The proprietor was L. Muggleston. There is a postbox in the wall and advertisements for Fry's, Cadbury's and Rowntree's Chocolate.

The National Schools were built in 1841 and used until 1929, after which they were demolished.

the same year plans were drawn up for the sale of a considerable amount of land from the estate of Colonel Craddock. Proposals for Knighton Park were included in the plan, together with a large number of building plots, many of which were purchased by local architects and builders. A number of the roads on the original plan had been named, one of which was Battenburg Avenue. During World War One the name was changed to Carisbrooke Road. By the time the war began only a few houses had been built on the new road. In 1933 Carisbrooke Lawn Tennis Club was founded. Overdale Primary School, on Eastcourt Road, which opened in 1953, is recalled by one former pupil as housing a part-time public library in the basement. Southfields library and Knighton library on Clarendon Park Road were some distance away.

Even in the 1950s and 1960s a childhood in West Knighton was idyllic. Palmerston Boulevard was a cul-de-sac, like many roads in the area, and no major road linked the Welford and London roads. There were wide expanses of uncultivated grassland on the edges of the more formal Knighton Park and Knighton Spinney, where the local children spent carefree summer holidays building 'dens' and generally enjoying childhood in the same way that the village children had done 50 years and more before them. There were also the pleasures of the Kenwood open-air swimming pool on a hot summer's day. The pool was eventually sold to build more housing, despite protests from 2,000 residents who much preferred the pool.

Building continued in Knighton into the 1990s with the *Leicester Mercury* writing on 16 January 1992 of protests that a mediaeval ridge and furrow system would be destroyed and damage caused to a conservation area if the building of 12 substantial luxury houses went ahead. Knighton is still a leafy middle-class area, but today many of the grand houses are university halls of residence.

The Craddock Arms, c.1880, when the landlord was John Sibson.

The spacious gabled semi-detached houses of New Knighton in 1908. The National Schools are in the background.

Mr Rodwell delivering milk, with Newmarket Street in the background, c.1890.

An early photograph of Knighton Road, with St Mary's Church in the background.

The poplars on the old Knighton Road.

The Post Office and the Craddock Arms. The car is late 1920s.

Old cottages in the snow in Chapel Lane, c.1890.

A very rural picture of Knighton, a hundred years ago.

Knighton a century ago.

Knighton Road, cottages and gas lamps in the early 20th century.

Chapel Lane, early 1960s.

Chapel Lane, c.1920s.

Knighton Fields

Knighton Fields is the area to the west of Knighton and Clarendon Park formerly known as part of the Kirby Estate. The land reputedly once formed part of the Craddock Estate. Before the area began to be built up in the 1880s, mainly by Orson Wright, land agent and builder, the only building in the area was the solid and comfortable-looking Knighton Fields House, dating from around 1845, said to have been built for John Johnson who died in 1877. By 1914 the house was home to the honorary curate of St James's in Aylestone Park, the Lord Revd David Williams. In 1888 Cecil Ogden, architect of the Grand Hotel, drew up plans for 16 houses to be built on land next to the Knighton Junction Brickworks. The area was known as the Storks Head Estate, taking its name from the nearby public house on the Welford Road, near to Westbury Road. This is now the New Road Inn, and this part of Welford Road was referred to as Wigston Lane at the end of the 19th century.

The red-brick church of St Michael and All Angels in Scott Street was designed by Everard and Pick in 1897–8 and cost £4,500 to build. It became a separate parish in 1930. Like many churches in the late 20th century, St Michael's became redundant and closed in 1994. The block of flats that now occupies the site where the church stood has the church's foundation stone inset into the brickwork. The interesting rectangular vicarage, with its Swithland slate roof, was built in 1934–5, replacing an earlier building. It is still in use as a private house. Everard and Pick also designed the parish hall and schools on the corner of Stanfell and Welford roads in around 1900. This was another red-brick building, rather plain, almost severe, but using the local Swithland slate for the roof and incorporating a small garden in the initial plan. Three schoolrooms occupied the ground floor and the hall was above.

The area was and still is dominated by the Leicester Co-operative Wholesale Society's giant Wheatsheaf Works shoe factory, opened in 1894, with a foundation stone of 1891 inset in the brickwork. This magnificent red-brick building, with an imposing clocktower, is a symbol of the success of Leicester's boot and shoe industry in its heyday.

In 1925, when parts of the estate were sold, Knighton Fields House and lodges were valued at £2,500. The house had five bedrooms and three dressing rooms. The vicar of St Mary's Church in Knighton received 12 shillings a year in tithes and the Ecclesiastical Commissioners were paid a corn rent of £20 14s 6d annually from the estate. Knighton Fields House was let and the tenant, a Mr Johnson, was not too pleased that the neighbouring farmland was being sold to build local authority housing, not to mention the disruption caused by all the building work. He wrote to his new landlords, the Borough of Leicester Council, asking for his rent of £210 per annum to be reduced to

Knighton Fields House as it looks in 2003.

£125 per annum because of his altered surroundings. The council suggested £180, but the tenant would only agree to £150. The rent on the very ornate lodge on the Welford Road was 8 shillings a week. In building the new estate some damage was caused to Mr Johnson's pigsty, and the council agreed to re-erect it and put up a boundary fence. In 1930 Leicester Corporation had Knighton Fields House considerably extended to designs by J.O. Thompson and it became the Leicester College of Domestic Science. The main house is now Millgate School and the former Domestic Science college extension is now used by Leicester and Leicestershire Arts in Education, providing the city and county with a centre of excellence in music, dance and drama.

A number of the new local authority houses, particularly on Herrick Road, were built to Arthur Wakerley's economic £299 design. Tenants of the Kirby Estate were also provided with allotments. Knighton Fields West Primary School was opened in 1928 to serve the newly expanded area and in 1937 Sir Jonathon North Girls' School opened on Knighton Lane, followed by Lancaster Boys' School in 1960.

Knighton Fields remains a relatively small suburb and has been virtually the same size since the 1920s. Several of the roads in the area were named after famous writers, including Herrick Road, although the Herricks were also a well-known Leicester family. In 1937 the Knighton Kinema, with a seating capacity of almost 1,300, opened on the corner of Keble Road and Welford Road. It closed in 1963 and the site is now occupied by commercial premises. A hundred years ago this stretch of the Welford Road, from Victoria Park Road to Knighton Fields Road East, consisted mainly of housing and open fields. Today it is a busy shopping area, with a number of specialist shops, together with a cosmopolitan spread of restaurants and an additional public house.

Mowmacre Hill

One of Mowmacre Hill's claims to fame is the Battle of Mowmacre Hill. During the early 1840s there had been much political unrest, there was mass unemployment and many people were on the brink of starvation. In August 1842 there were numerous strikes, initially in the north and in the neighbouring county of Staffordshire. The miners in Leicestershire were the first to go on strike, followed by other workers who disrupted the town centre with various processions and attempts to persuade others to join them. They were greatly influenced by a passionate Chartist, Thomas Cooper, whose charismatic speeches fuelled their actions. One group went on strike and held a meeting in Humberstone Gate on 19 August 1842. Their grievance was that despite only being able to work for half a week they still had to pay a week's rent for the use of the framework knitting machines, which were used in their homes, in addition to feeding their families. The group intended to march to Loughborough to meet with other protestors, stopping at Belgrave on the way. As they approached Mowmacre Hill they were prevented from going further by Frederick Goodyer, the chief of the county

Mowmacre Hill in Belgrave Parish, 1918–20.

Mowmacre Hill, looking up the hill to the 19th-century house on the right, late 1950s or early 1960s.

Thurcaston Road, with the railway at the end, late 1950s or early 1960s.

police force, together with the constabulary and yeomanry. The strike was over in a few days and Colin Ellis in *History in Leicester* writes that the event: '... was remembered in the best possible way, as a joke against both sides.' He also notes rather amusingly: '... there was one casualty of a sort, during a night patrol of the streets ... This "casualty" resulted, even many years after the event, in any of the Yeomanry Cavalry being spotted on the streets of Leicester being met with a cry of: "Who shot the pump?"'

Until the 1950s Mowmacre Hill was little more than the name of the hill that was part of Thurcaston Lane and formed the footpath to Birstall. It was part of Beaumont parish but was in the postal area of Belgrave. It was a popular place in the 19th century for a Sunday afternoon stroll or a cycle ride, with views over open fields in one direction and the town in the other. There were a handful of houses on Mowmacre Hill in the early 20th century, as well as the British United Athletic Ground and Birstall Golf Club. During the 1950s approximately 1,300 council houses were built there. As with many new local authority estates, the houses were built first and a community centre and shops were added a few years later.

Thurcaston Road with the railway bridge at the end and an old 30 miles per hour speed limit sign.

The busy thoroughfare of Mowmacre Hill, with mid to late 19th-century houses on either side, c.1890.

Mowmacre Hill, c.1890.

New Parks

New Parks was formerly part of Leicester Forest and situated in a sizeable area called the Frith. It first became known as New Parks after it was enclosed in 1526, at which time it was also made an extra-parochial area. In the 14th century a foresters' lodge existed and was referred to as Byrdes-Nest Lodge. In 1377–8 major repairs were carried out and it survived for almost a century and a half before being renovated again in 1525–6. The lodge was surveyed in 1560 and valued at £25 13s 4d. Included in the valuation were seven 'chymnes', valued at 3s 4d each. Despite the renovations, after New Parks was enclosed it fell out of use and was left to deteriorate, although it survived in some form until the 18th century. The building had a particularly fine quadrangular moat with a drawbridge and was reputed to be the hunting lodge of John of Gaunt. It was also known as John of Gaunt's summer house. There could have been little left when John Throsby visited in 1790 and noted: 'Near this is a place called Birds Nest, formerly the dwelling of some man of consequence; the house was moated, which now remains visible.' The moat survived until the land was required for building in 1950, and the name is commemorated in Birds Nest Avenue. Birds Nest Farm and Birds Nest Cottage appear on a block plan of 1888, drawn up by Everard and Pick. The Glenfield railway tunnel is also marked on the plan and the land to the east of Birds Nest Farm belonged to Captain Aikman, another name to be found on the New Parks Estate.

A view down Bonney Road from the White House School in 1951.

An aerial view of the estate in 1969.

An incomplete St Aidan's Church in 1955.

Leicester Forest belonged to the Duchy of Lancaster and after the enclosure of New Parks there were proposals to lease or rent out the area, which would yield £70 7s 6d per annum. In 1550 William Parr, Marquis of Northampton, was granted the land from the Crown, although he was obliged to return the land in 1553 because of a felony. William, Lord Cobham, held the property from 1571, but the land must have been fated, because his descendant Henry Lord Cobham, who like Parr committed a serious crime, caused it once again to revert to the Crown. Several more people owned it for brief periods before William Mitchell, who is said to have died in 1745 leaving the property of New Parks. From 1781 to 1843 it was owned by the Clarke family. In 1830 John Clarke was recorded as the principal landowner, the area then consisting of 815 acres, two rods and 30 perches.

By the mid-19th century the major holder of the land was John Mellor, a judge, who later became Sir John. His father, also John, was mayor of Leicester in 1844. Two hosiery manufacturers owned most of the remainder; these were Thomas Stokes, for whom New Parks House was built in 1845–46, and J.O. Harris. The area remained largely agricultural until the end of the 19th century and was sparsely populated with two houses and three people being recorded in 1801. Seventy years later there were 69 people and 11 houses. After Sir John Mellor's death, his family sold 170 acres of the estate to Leicester

New Parks House School pictured in 1951, when it was not quite completed.

Corporation in 1897, for use as a public park. The Mellor trustees sold the land for £28,500, a sum considerably less than its true value.

Between 1933 and 1937 Leicester Corporation purchased virtually all of the remaining land, with plans to build municipal housing. The onset of World War Two delayed this until 1945. Between 1946 and 1959 more than 3,000 houses were built in New Parks, including 500 steel-framed houses, which could be erected speedily. The growing housing shortage, together with the many thousands of houses condemned as slums, meant urgent answers were needed. A number of prefabricated buildings, known as 'prefabs', were constructed on the New Parks Estate. They were intended as a temporary measure to ease the housing shortage and were meant to have a lifespan of 10 years. They survived for far longer and were still in reasonable condition when the council decided their fate in 1970. Many tenants left with extreme reluctance and the prefabs are remembered with affection by many who lived in them.

Designs for buildings in New Parks received high acclaim, and the shops on Aikman Avenue were awarded the Royal Institute of British Architects bronze medal for being the most outstanding new buildings erected in Leicestershire and Rutland in 1950–57. The eminent architect Basil Spence, who also designed Coventry Cathedral, was chosen to design the church of St Aidan, New Parks, after a new ecclesiastical area was created in 1947. Work began in 1957. When the new church was completed in 1959, the

Moving into a new house in 1962. 162 houses were completed in 162 days, built by the contractors Sir Lindsay Parkinson and Co. Ltd. Because of the tremendous feat he entertained the men on the site the following Friday. Each house has a lounge, thee bedrooms and central heating.

Erratum

Page 121: the three photographs of Gooding Avenue should appear in the Braunstone chapter.

Gooding Avenue.

;ation expressed their dislike of the tower, finding it rather insubstantial, although ıade of concrete. Their comments finally reached the ears of Sir Basil Spence who, ;h much preferring his original design, agreed to produce an alternative to appease ics. The new design met with the parishioners' approval and was constructed within two weeks. The church has a copper roof and the open tower has coloured louvres, the overall design being one of simplicity. In the 21st century New Parks is still an area of wide green spaces, with many of the houses now being owner-occupied.

Two children outside their new homes in 1949.

Just across the Groby Road from New Parks is Leicester Frith. Like New Parks it was also extra-parochial. The Groby Road formed its southern boundary and from 1753 was a turnpike road, which meant a toll had to be paid to use it. Generally the turnpike roads were kept in better repair. In the 17th and 18th century the Frith was known as Sherman's Lodge or Sherman's Grounds, after the major family of landowners in the area, although it was also sometimes known as Markham's Close. In 1610 John Sherman had the land on lease from the Duchy of Lancaster and it continued to be held by the same family until the early 19th century. William Oldham, the Leicester architect and builder, then acquired the land from Mrs Elizabeth Sherman, in 1812 or 1813. Isaac Harrison, who lived in Newfoundpool House and owned the land in Newfoundpool, acquired Leicester Frith in 1861. A Leicester cotton manufacturer, Thomas Smith Taylor, owned much of the land by 1870. The land was held in trust after his death, and in 1909 Leicester Corporation bought 93 acres, followed by an additional 118 acres in 1919.

The small area was entirely agricultural and in 1811 had only one house and seven inhabitants. Although the population expanded it remained very small: in 1851 there were 33 people and 20 years later 47. Leicester Frith House was extended during World War One to accommodate soldiers suffering from shell shock, money being provided from the Lord Mayor's Fund. The hospital became known as the Leicester Frith Recovery Home and was used for servicemen until 1924. It was then used as a convalescent home and a hospital for the mentally ill.

NEWFOUNDPOOL

Little is known of the origins of Newfoundpool and it makes its first appearance on a map of 1828. It was an extra-parochial area and did not become part of the borough of Leicester until 1891. The land seems to have been owned by Isaac Harrison from around 1830. Harrison was associated with a market gardening company in Leicester. He found a spring on the land and hoped to make the area into a popular and profitable spa, since 'taking the waters' in places such as Bath and Ashby de la Zouch had been a fashionable pursuit for the wealthy since the 18th century. Harrison had a large house constructed where people could bathe and drink the spring water, and he employed a doctor and attendants. The venture was initially very popular but survived for only four or five years. Harrison then began to consider mining for coal on the site but this came to nothing and after alterations had been carried out he lived in the house himself. By 1845 his brother seems to have owned the land, at which time the Midland Railway, which was considering constructing a line in the area, had it surveyed. The property, which became known as Newfoundpool House, passed to a nephew, Isaac, and in turn to his daughter, Beatrice. Isaac Harrison also owned large tracts of land in north-east Leicester, which were sold to William Gray in 1877. Several roads were created in the developing suburb of Belgrave. Newfoundpool House, with later baronial additions, survives as the Empire Hotel. From 1920–1939, the landlord was Arthur Richard Cain. He was the grandson of bare-knuckle fighter Tom Cain, who in his brief five-year career in the ring was defeated only once.

A very early photograph of the Leicester–Swannington railway level crossing on Fosse Road North.

Leicester builder and land agent Orson Wright purchased the land in around 1885, laying out the roads and constructing some small houses, selling the remainder of the land as building plots. The name Isaac Harrison is to be found in the initials of the streets between Pool Road and Beatrice Road, making an acrostic. In 1891, when much of the area was complete, the census records 2,160 people residing there, although in 1881 there had been a mere 56. In 1891 Ingle Street Board School for infants and juniors opened and it is still there today. In 1897 the Fosse Infant and Secondary School opened in Mantle Road.

In 1894 the area became the ecclesiastical parish of St Augustine. An iron mission church had existed from 1888, when many of the houses were constructed. From 1900 the vast red-brick, almost barn-like structure of the church of St Augustine, with its superb Swithland slate roof, was erected on Fosse Road North. Designed by R.J. and J. Goodacre, a pleasant garden softened the almost severe building. Construction of the western part of the church was not completed until 1912. In the same year Everard and Pick drew up plans for a substantial vicarage, set in a landscaped garden near to the church. The incumbent at the time was the Revd John Casson. The vicarage was replaced with a contemporary building and all that remains of its predecessor are parts of the once extensive garden wall. The primitive Methodists had their chapel from St Nicholas Street, originally built in 1873, re-erected in Fosse Road North in 1898 when the site was acquired for the development of the Great Central Railway. The chapel was designed by James Kerridge (*c.*1830–1911), of Wisbech. In 1903, Leicester architect Samuel Henry Langley added the chapel Sunday Schools. Sadly the chapel is no longer in use and planning permission is being sought to build a number of flats on the site.

The Fosse Cinema opened in 1936 and, after it had closed as a cinema, spent the latter part of its life echoing to the cry of the bingo caller. It was finally demolished in the 1990s to make way for a garage and small store owned by Tesco. The Leicester Co-operative Society had their stables in the area and the sign and part of the buildings, now workshops, may still be seen. On the corner of Tudor Road and Fosse Road North is a fine example of a Co-operative grocery store, executed in an exuberant Arts and Crafts style, with a dominant half-timbered gable. Fosse Road North, as well as being a busy shopping area, also has some fine three and four-storey red-brick villas. One of the *Leicester Mercury*'s longest serving editors, Harry Hackett, lived at No.354 in 1914. Interestingly, in 1902 James Thompson, manager of the *Post*, *Chronicle* and *Mercury*, lived next door at No.356, and Mrs Florence Thompson was still there in 1914. Jimmy Thompson, as he was known, described in Steve England's book as a 'genial Scot', died in 1913, having been manager of the *Mercury* for 36 years. The different newspapers were both forerunners of today's *Leicester Mercury*. Harry Hackett spent 45 years of his working life at the *Mercury*, 33 as editor. He was a staunch Liberal and was on the committee of the Leicester West constituency at the time Winston Churchill stood as the

Liberal candidate in 1923. Churchill lost the election and switched his political allegiance to the Conservative party.

Most of the housing in Newfoundpool was terraced but much of it has a wide variety of decorative elements. The artisan's houses on Oban Street have elegant leaded bays and tiny front gardens. Devon House in Newport Street, an exceptionally pleasant example, was occupied at the beginning of World War One by a lady music teacher, who had trained at the Royal Academy of Music in London. A number of the spacious corner premises, providing shop and living accommodation, had more unusual and elaborate features. The shop on the corner of Newport Street and Beatrice Road still has its miniscule balcony with iron railings. In the early part of the 20th century it was a furniture shop.

For many years residents of Newfoundpool had the countryside on their doorstep, as the area was surrounded on three sides by fields and allotments until the small Freake's Ground Estate was constructed in 1934–5. This was followed by a further local authority estate, New Parks, begun shortly after the end of World War Two. For many years people living in the area also had to put up with the clatter of trains steaming over the nearby railway bridge. The 11 acres which comprised the Fosse Recreation Ground opened in the year of Queen Victoria's Diamond Jubilee in 1897. It was complete with the obligatory bandstand and just in time for the Jubilee celebrations.

Writing about his memories of the area in the 1930s, G. Miles notes the wonderful variety of tempting aromas that assailed you when shopping in the area. Bacon joints were to be had at King's the grocers, Sibsons the butchers had hot roast pork and beer intermingled with the smell of polished mahogany. Today it is still a busy area – although many corner shops struggle to survive there are still a large number in Newfoundpool. A number of small businesses still occupy the late 19th-century factory premises and workshops.

Adjacent to Newfoundpool, and similarly a separate civil parish until 1891, was Freake's Ground. It had been part of Leicester Forest and was probably enclosed before 1526. Henry, Earl of Huntingdon, owned it in 1577 and in 1589 it was purchased by one of Leicester's major butchers, Philip Freake. In 1625 Leicester Corporation bought the land from Freake's son, John. The area was largely agricultural and it is likely that Philip Freake, with his sizeable butchery establishment, used it as grazing land. The area also had a windmill which survived until the late 19th century.

In 1871 Leicester Corporation erected an isolation or fever hospital on two acres of the land. The hospital was used for appalling and virulent diseases like smallpox, and its opening almost coincided with a smallpox epidemic in Leicester in which 346 people died, some of whom had been vaccinated. From 1867 it became compulsory to have babies vaccinated against smallpox before they were three months old. A great deal of suspicion still surrounded preventative medicine and many Leicester people refused to

The other side of the Fosse Road North level crossing, again a very early photograph.

have their children vaccinated, which resulted in a fine or a prison sentence. Amos Booth (1843–1926), a Leicester Venetian blind manufacturer, championed the anti-vaccination cause and defended many of those brought to court. Isolating the patients was another way of preventing the spread of the disease and this became known as the Leicester Method. The corrugated iron buildings were extended in 1893 but had become obsolete by 1900 when a new hospital was opened at Gilroes. One of the original lodges still remains on Fosse Lane. Much of the former Freake's Ground is still in the ownership of the city council. A small part of the New Parks Estate was built on some of the land, while the remainder stayed as allotments. The allotments provided gardens for the shopkeepers and business people who literally 'lived over the shop' and had only tiny back yards. A tiny brick garden hut dating from the 1860s is still there as a reminder of the days when people would spend a weekend or bank holiday on their allotment. This rather charming 19th-century building remained in a reasonable state of repair for many years. Despite being granted listed building status a few years ago, it has been the subject of vandalism and has sadly deteriorated considerably.

Further reading:

England, Steve, *Magnificent Mercury History of a Regional Newspaper: The First 125 Years of the Leicester Mercury*, Kaiross Press, 1999.

Saffron Lane Estate

The area now known as the Saffron Lane Estate was once part of the parish of Aylestone and for a number of years the road of Saffron Lane was the site of a gibbet. It could be used as a gallows and was also a post on which the bodies of criminals were hung to deter others. Benjamin Goodman, Chamberlain Clerk to the Poor Law Guardians for many years, records in his diary of 1832 that 'Cook the binder' was hung at the Infirmary and then 'elevated on a gibbet in Saffron Lane'. When the Saffron Lane Estate was first built in the 1920s it was known by the rather imposing name of the Park Estate. The name, which had an air of gentility, never quite caught on and the area was always referred to as the Saffron Lane Estate or more colloquially as 'The Saff'. In the aftermath of World War One there was a desperate housing shortage, and the Government and the Leicester Corporation were much preoccupied with providing 'Homes fit for Heroes'. The solution was to provide as much local authority housing as possible, and in Leicester Saffron Lane was the first major council estate constructed after the war. Land for the new estate was purchased from Colonel Craddock, who had been selling off considerable quantities of his vast estate (stretching from Knighton Fields to Aylestone) since the 1900s. At the same time another wealthy landowner, Mrs Eyres Monsell, sold part of her Leicestershire estates. Approximately 79 acres were purchased in February 1923 for £18,169. In April 1924 a further 169 acres were purchased from Mrs Eyres Monsell for £22,350 and in January 1925 Colonel Craddock sold a further portion of his estate.

Meadow Gardens, Saffron Lane Estate, 1982.

By May 1924 the list of people applying for council housing had reached 5,700 and the Corporation was under pressure to build these as quickly as possible. A labour shortage in the construction industry led the council to approve the building of 1,500 concrete houses by Messrs Henry Boot and Son (London) Ltd. Despite some reservations, and the fact that it cost £465 for a concrete non-parlour house as opposed to £395 for a brick house, building went ahead. In an attempt to alleviate the rather monotonous design of the 'Boot' houses, different colours were used for roof tiles and a variety of shades for the

Elston Fields, Saffron Lane Estate, 1995.

A steam engine on the site of the old level crossing, 1960.

Saffron Lane, a shepherd with his sheep after a blizzard, 31 March 1916.

roughcast rendered exteriors. Although it was possible to build more quickly using this method, problems began to emerge not long after the houses were built, with cracks appearing in the concrete foundations. The houses survived until the 1990s when the last

Saffron Lane after the blizzard on 31 March 1916. Note the van driver is female.

one was demolished on 5 June 1997. Despite the council's initial ambitious plans for many amenities including a railway station, it was some time before even a doctor's surgery or shops materialised. The estate followed a garden city layout with curving roads, green open spaces and generous gardens for leisure and cultivating fruit and vegetables. The estate was laid out around the park of Elston Fields, which the locals referred to as 'Tick-Tock Park'. The pavilion boasted a clocktower.

Marriott Road School was the first one on the new estate. Temporary wooden huts were provided for the first influx of nursery children and in 1927 an infant and junior school was built. The school was officially opened on 9 March 1928 by the Chairman of the City Education Committee, Sir Jonathon North, who was to give his name to another Leicester school. There was space for approximately 750 children. The *Daily Mail*, reporting on the event that evening, noted that the cost of building on the four and a half acre site was in the region of £27,323. Concerns about health and fresh air meant that the single-storey building had French windows and verandahs to provide as much sunlight as possible, and lawns and flowerbeds completed the picture. Southfields Drive School followed in 1926, originally as a temporary junior school known as Lubbesthorpe Park Temporary Junior Council School, after the parish of the same name. Children from both the city and county attended. Buildings and equipment presented a number of problems until a new building was completed in January 1934. The area was expanding rapidly as more houses in the inner city were demolished and further schools were needed. The Newry School opened in 1932 and the Linwood Lane Schools for senior age children in

Making the new bypass on Saffron Lane, January 1932.

1928. In 1958 the latter became a boys' school and Mary Linwood School for girls opened on Trennant Road. The Linwood Lane Boys' School closed in 1983, but pressure from local residents saved the building and it was reopened as a community centre in 1986. Holy Cross Roman Catholic Primary School, which had previously been in New Walk, moved to a new building in Stonesby Avenue and was opened by the Bishop of Nottingham, the Right Revd E. Ellis, on 26 September 1967.

The new population of the Park Estate needed transport and this was supplied from 1925 onwards by Leicester Corporation's new motor buses. A temporary Church of England was provided in an old barn. *The Story of the Saff* records that the barn was not without its problems: 'A choir boasting 22 members was gathered together. Eventually an average attendance of 100 was secured for church services, including "The Barn Cat" and a cockerel.' The cat was also inclined to enter the church in the middle of prayers and sermons. Having entered, it often could not find a way out and would meow loudly until someone let it out. In 1928 the church of St Christopher on Marriott Road, designed by William Keay, was opened, to serve both as a church and hall in one. Forty years later the opening of a new church, designed by the Roger Keene Partnership, was reported in the *Leicester Mercury* on 9 May 1968. The cost of the new building was £22,500. The previous

Saffron Lane level crossing in 1928.

church now serves as the church hall. The Roman Catholic Church of St John Bosco, Stonesby Avenue, opened in 1936. A new church of the same name was later to be built on the Eyres Monsell Estate. On the social side of the Saffron Lane Estate a Working Men's Club on Duncan Road opened in 1929. There were no pubs on the estate and the club was an important part of the social life of the area, providing a room for children, concerts and outings.

A branch of Worthington's on the corner of St Andrews Road and Saffron Lane and a Co-op on The Fairway initially served the new estate, with many other shops following. It was to be some years before the estate had its own library; a temporary wooden building behind the Post Office in Southfields Drive was the first facility for borrowing books. A classroom in Southfields Drive School was the next library venue, serving both the city and the county. At the end of the 1930s Leicester architects Symington, Prince and Pike designed Southfields Branch Library, complete with a 200-seat lecture theatre. In 1946 the architects won the Royal Institute of British Architects bronze medal for the best building erected during the previous decade (1936–1946). The circular shape is reminiscent of several of London's 1930s tube stations. It reminds Leicester folk of a pork pie, and it is often referred to as the 'Pork Pie Library'! It was a very welcome addition to

Saffron Lane at the junction with Wigston Lane, late 1950s or early 1960s.

the neighbourhood and officially opened in July 1939, just before the outbreak of World War Two. Affectionate childhood memories of the new library just after the war are recorded in *The Story of the Saff.* One lady recalled that books and paper were still rationed and queues would form to reserve new books. She also delighted in the warmth of the building and the thrill of reading the weekly children's comics.

New houses have replaced the Boot homes and the remainder have all been refurbished over the years. The Saff has now been in existence for almost 80 years and is still going strong. Saffron Lane itself is a busy shopping area.

Further reading:

The Story of the Saff, Leicester City Council, The Living History Unit, 1998.

Willbond, Bill, *A Home of Our Own: 70 Years of Council House Memories in Leicester*, Leicester City Council, 1991.

Spinney Hills

Mere Road, which runs along the west side of Spinney Hill Park, was no more than a rough track until the late 19th century when the area began to be developed. Mere was the term used for a boundary and until the borough boundary was extended in 1891 Mere Road was just that, the dividing line between town and county. The view from this high vantage point was one of fields across to the brick pits that would eventually become Melbourne Road. Spinney Hill Park was opened on 24 August 1886 by the wife of the mayor, Israel Hart. She was presented with a bejewelled gold key to mark the event, which was attended by 400 people. The occasion was also marked by a firework display presented by Mr W. Carr, 'Pyrotechnist', of Wharf Street, Leicester. The 36 acres of land, purchased in the previous year for £18,000, had been the property of the Burnaby family. J.F.L. Rolleston, who was Burnaby's agent, handled the sale. He was later to become Sir John Rolleston, together with being MP for the borough of Leicester at the turn of the century. Sir John was also well acquainted with Orson Wright, a noted builder and land agent, who had a hand in many of Leicester's suburban developments. The name Spinney Hill Park arose from the fact that the area was surrounded by small spinneys, together with the proximity of Spinney Hill Farm. H. Simpson Gee, of the Stead and Simpson footwear family, reminiscing on her childhood in the 1870s, remembers sharing a field that is now part of the park with the family of the major Leicester architect, Joseph Goddard. She recalls there being a summerhouse where they had tea, and a pony for the children to ride.

Spinney Hill Park, 1905. Girls in clean white pinafores on a postcard sent to Miss Ida Spencer, who lived not too far from the park, at 49 Myrtle Road.

Children playing with hoops on Spinney Hill Park, 1909.

Spinney Hill Park, c.1914.

In the year the park was opened Spencer's Guide commented that it was: 'The most agreeable and popular of our public resorts'; going on to praise in particular 'a handsome fountain of polished granite.' The park had wonderful views over the eastern side of the town and across to Crown Hills, and it also possessed that prerequisite of all Victorian parks, a bandstand. Music, particularly brass band music with a military touch, was immensely popular entertainment on Sunday afternoons and bank holidays, remaining so until the 1950s. In winter the slopes of Spinney Hill Park provided a superb area for sledging. The park had a sizeable pavilion, which was added in 1888 at a cost of £609 19s. A keeper's lodge was built in the same year, costing £319 18s. The pavilion restaurant was remembered as providing good quality meals at reasonable prices in the 1930s. During World War One, like a number of other parks in the city, several areas were planted with potatoes to supplement the limited supply of vegetables available.

The park was situated in an ideal spot for the residents close to the park. One of the

Spinney Hill Park, just before World War One. A uniformed nanny with a large perambulator is in the foreground.

roads was initially designed with the rear of the houses facing the park but this was met with some controversy, as R.G. Waddington wrote in *The Illustrated Leicester Chronicle* of 18 April 1931: 'There was such an outcry against this that Park Vale Road was mapped out, running along the south side of the park.' Building continued over the next three decades with some very pleasing designs by the notable Leicester architect and councillor, Arthur Wakerley (1862–1931). Wakerley had already designed a number of houses on Mere Road at the end of the 19th century and in 1910 he produced a design for 10 spacious four-bedroomed terraced houses on East Park Road opposite the park, complete with a row of lime trees. The *Midland Free Press* of 3 June 1911 commented: 'We have not seen examples of modern houses in Leicester so well worth visiting for inspection as these cheap and charming residences on the East Park Road.' The expanding suburb also obscured a sizeable moat, which had been visible until the end of the 19th century; Moat Road takes its name from this former historic landmark.

Spinney Hill Park is still there today, serving a diverse, multicultural community.

Further reading:

Beazley, B., *Four Years Remembered: Leicester During the Great War*, Breedon Books Publishing Company Ltd, 1999.

Ellis, I.C., *Nineteenth Century Leicester*, published by the author, 1935.

Leicester City Council, *Spinney Hill Park Centenary, 1886–1986*, Leicester City Council, 1986.

Spinney Hill Park. The poster advertises a performance of the Messiah by the 500 voices of the Methodist Choir, in the late 1920s or early 1930s.

Stoneygate

The name Stoneygate is derived from Stonegate, which the Leicester to Medbourne Road was known as in 1515. Late in the 17th century the first house was built on the Harborough Road and was likely to have been a farmhouse. This house was known as the Stoney Gate, with or without the 'e'. Some time around 1780 it was remodelled in Gothic fashion. The gables were raised and the exterior was encased in red brick. Further extensions and alterations took place over the next 20 or 30 years. From 1846 it was the home of Major William Freer who was Clerk of the Peace for Leicestershire, and his descendants lived there until until 1945. The house was unfortunately demolished in 1962.

The solidly middle-class suburb of Stoneygate has its origins in the 18th century, when it is suggested that the first house to be built there since the 17th century, in about 1760, was Stoneygate House, on Toller Road. Toller Road was then the main turnpike road from Market Harborough to Loughborough. The house had many illustrious owners: Samuel Oliver, who was mayor of Leicester, was said to have been the first. By 1846, Stoneygate House had become the property of Thomas Nunneley, a grocer. Richard Toller, a hosiery manufacturer, was the next purchaser, and the company of Lankester and Toller was situated on Jarrom Street. In 1896 the estate was sold and Burlington Road and Southernhay Road began to be developed. The name of the Toller family is commemorated in Toller Road. There were several other owners, including Josiah and Kingsley Gimson, who resided there for a few years from 1913. They were respectively director and director and secretary of Gimson and Co. (Leicester) Ltd. The house, like many substantial old properties, was demolished in the 1950s. John Biggs (1801–1871), the nonconformist Liberal who was three times mayor of Leicester, rather confusingly had the Stoneygate built in about 1845. He fell upon hard times, selling the property in 1862. He moved briefly to Portland House near the borough boundary and later in much reduced circumstances to a terraced house on the Welford Road. Biggs, whose statue is to be found in Welford Place, was also a philanthropist and entrepreneur. He and his brother William were said to be the major employers in the hosiery industry in the 19th century.

White's Directory, published in 1846, records 10 properties in Stoneygate. John Biggs had moved to a house on the land that is now Knighton Park Road, while Charles Robinson, the owner of the Leicester Gas Works, lived in the The Shrubbery, the gardens of which were designed by Sir Joseph Paxton. Paxton was also an architect and designed the Crystal Palace for the Great Exhibition held in 1851. In 1848 Samuel Stone had Elmfield built. He was the Town Clerk for many years and also wrote *Stone's Justices Manual*, a work still in use today. Brookfield was built in 1846 for the Burgess family and

The Stoneygate, Toller Road, demolished in the 1960s. The neat shrubs contrast with the sorry dilapidation of the house.

later occupied by Thomas Fielding Johnson, one of Leicester's major hosiery manufacturers. Mrs Agnes Fielding Johnson was a local historian. In 1891 she wrote *Glimpses of Ancient Leicester in Six Periods.* A further edition was published in 1906.

Portland House, its pleasing and comfortable façade reached via a long driveway, is now Leicester High School for Girls. It was said to have been built in 1826 as a hunting lodge for the Duke of Portland. H. Herbert bought it in the 1920s, then sold it to Mr and Mrs Holles, who opened it as a school in 1926. Mrs Emily Holles had already been running a small private school at 10, Alexandra Road, Stoneygate for some years, while Thomas Holles was the head of Lansdowne Road Boys' Secondary School in Aylestone Park. Further down the London Road, in what is now Grenfell Road, are a number of 19th-century houses. In the early years of the 20th century Harry Peach (1874–1936) lived at No.1 Portland Towers. Harry Hardy Peach, a former bookseller, founded the Dryad Company in 1907, with Benjamin Fletcher, who was Head of the Leicester School of Art. In 1914 he was living at Ashover in Knighton Road. The Dryad Company, which produced cane furniture and 'art metalwork', rapidly achieved national acclaim. Peach was also a founder member of the Design and Industries Association in 1915. Their first exhibition was held in several major cities, including Leicester.

The sale of the D'Oyly Estate in 1858 opened up more land for development and speculative builders and freehold land societies began to buy up plots in the area. From about 1865 the side roads were laid out. In 1859 G.B. Franklin opened a school which still survives today as Stoneygate School. The school had a series of distinguished headmasters. The school was fondly remembered by 'Oz', the pseudonym of the Reverend Cecil Osmond Tabberer (1889–1971) who lived at The Holt, just a few doors away on London Road. His father, George Osmond, was part of the firm of Pool, Lorrimer and Tabberer, hosiery manufacturers and worsted spinners, who had premises in King Street and Welford Road. In the *Leicester Mercury* of 22 February 1961, Oz recalls: 'I first went to Stoneygate School in the year of Queen Victoria's Diamond Jubilee, 1897. It was then Miss Franklin's School and Miss Constance Franklin assisted.' Shortly after the eight-year-old Osmond joined the school, the Miss Franklins retired, to be replaced by George Edward Rudd, who was always known as 'Boss'. Oz wrote with affection of the Boss's

Town End Close, Ratcliffe Road, pictured in 1948, when it was purchased for £8,500 to be converted to a hall of residence for students of the Domestic Science College.

history lessons, declaring; 'They were sheer delight' and noted, 'What jolly masters we often had' – so much for the rigours of 19th-century male education! He writes too of his fellow school friends. The list is rather like a *Who's Who* of the sons of Leicester's manufacturers and entrepreneurs. In another article from the *Leicester Mercury* on 20 February 1961, Oz recalls his boyhood home, The Holt, part of the garden of which was sold to build Holmfield Road. A few years later the Tabberers left and in 1909 the house was demolished. The site became part of the garden of Brookfield. Oz wrote of the brook at the bottom of the field and said that a rhododendron bed marked the site of his former home.

The Lodge, on London Road was the home of Arthur Wakerley's parents-in-law, Thomas and Selina Gunn, for at least 30 years, Thomas Gunn was a manufacturer of ladies' ribbed underwear, with a factory in Crafton Street. He died in 1915 and the sale particulars of that year describe the house as a 'Substantial Family Residence'. The situation of the nine-bedroomed house, with stable block, paddock, greenhouse and aviary, as well as extensive gardens, is given as 'Occupying a pleasant position on the London Road, near to Toller Road, and within 15 minutes of the centre of Leicester by the electric cars.'

Virtually all the residents of Stoneygate were men and women of property; they were the town's manufacturers and professionals. Any history of the area is rather akin to a mass biography of the most eminent citizens of the borough of Leicester. Well over a century of architectural history is to be found here too, from mid-Victorian solidity to elegant Arts and Crafts, particularly in the Edwardian period (1901–1910). Morland Avenue delights in some very fine examples, with work by eminent Leicester architect Stockdale Harrison (1846–1914). Although a number of the original houses are no longer there, many still are. A few blocks of flats have infiltrated but the area still exudes leafy middle-class suburbia at its finest.

An Art Deco house with polychrome brickwork, in Southernhay Road.

Further reading:

Boynton, H. and D. Seaton, *From Tollgate to Tramshed: The History of London Road, Leicester c.1860–1920*, published by the authors, 1999.

Elliot, M., *Victorian Leicester*, Phillimore, 1979.

Thornton, P., *The Stoneygate Story*, published by the author, 1986.

Westcotes

The area known as Westcotes formed part of what was known as Bromkinsthorpe or Bruntingthorpe and was listed in the Domesday Book of 1086. At this date the spelling was 'Brunechinestorp' or, in Old English, 'Brunskinn', and it is thought to mean 'the thorpe of the brown skins'. Although the area was isolated by the River Soar, it was always part of the borough of Leicester. The land was divided into two areas under the Enclosure Acts during the reign of Charles I in 1626. Some 106 acres of land were allotted to the freeholders and cottagers, while 76 acres were given to Walter Ruding of Westcotes and 25 to his neighbour, John Danet of Danet's Hall. The Danets came to live at the hall in the 13th century and their descendants continued to live there until the 17th century. At the beginning of the 18th century John Watts bought the hall and had it rebuilt. It was one of the earliest houses in Leicester to be remodelled using brick. Although brick had been used earlier, notably on Leicester Castle, it was still relatively modern for the time and only the gentry could afford to use such costly material. The hall was situated

Hinckley Road at the junction of Westcotes Drive and Kirby Road in 1960. The substantial houses and shops, including a branch of Worthington's, were demolished over 20 years ago. Worthington's also had a shop at No.42 Hinckley Road.

Hinckley Road, just past the junction with Narborough Road and Braunstone Gate. North's Travel Agents is on the corner of Cranmer Street, while Harry North's butchers shop is on the corner of Ridley Street.

between Bow Bridge and Fosse Road on a wooded lane known as Watt's causeway, later to become King Richard's Road.

John Watts was an enlightened physician who later became a clergyman; he suggested that an infirmary should be opened in the town. His daughter, Susannah, wrote *A Walk Through Leicester* in 1804, which is still in print. Danet's Hall was sold in 1769 and had several owners before it was finally bought by another doctor, Joseph Noble, probably some time in the 1840s. Dr Noble was held in high regard by his professional colleagues and the local townsfolk, and in 1859, also the year of a general election, he became mayor. He was also a Liberal MP. Dr Noble certainly lived up to his name: he was apparently most hospitable and the hall was home to a number of refugees. Alice Hobson, whose house was opposite Danet's Hall, recalls in *Nineteenth Century Leicester* the 'sea of white blossoms' which was Dr Noble's cherry orchard, and she hid behind the buttresses of the high walls to his grounds, 'to pounce out on father when we went to meet him returning from the factory.' In the same book the young Miss Franklin remembered a party at the hall in the 1850s. Despite the delights of the party she notes, as only a child might, that the drive in a four-wheeler 'was very tiresome – starched white muslin, bows of ribbon, shawls etc.'

It was while Dr Noble was in residence that an archaeological dig took place in the cherry orchard next to the hall. In the early 1780s some Roman mosaics had been found among the cherry tree roots. A drawing was made and the mosaics were covered over and forgotten about. In 1850 Dr Noble, on discovering that he had Roman antiquities in his cherry orchard, offered to present them to the Town Hall, if they could be found! No one, however, had thought to mark the site of the first dig some 70 years previously! The orchard comprised 10–12 acres of land. In the spring of 1851, the Leicester Literary and Philosophical Society began their search in earnest. Using an iron probe they eventually came across part of a superb Roman pavement, completely different, however, to the drawing of the one made 70 years previously. Trenches were dug in all directions and they eventually began to uncover an entire Roman villa, the floors of which were almost completely covered in mosaics. The one discovered and drawn in 1783 still proved elusive and it was not until

The former Toll House on Hinckley Road, which stood on the crown of the hill just beyond Fosse Road. The house was purchased and rebuilt a few miles along the same road in Kirby Muxloe, where it still stands today.

A postcard sent to Kathleen Ward, who lived in Westcotes Drive in 1907. The postcard is an invitation to tea, and it is delightfully annotated with drawings of cakes, teacups, a cat and tiny mice.

Hinckley Road in the 1900s.

almost the entire villa had been unearthed that the paving that had initiated their search was revealed. They were delighted to have finally found it and great care was taken to protect it, with policemen guarding it day and night. There were just as many vandals and burglars in Victorian Leicester as there are today. The mosaic was finally taken in great state to the Town Hall and is now to be found in the Jewry Wall Museum.

In 1861 Dr Noble went on a visit to Spain and much to his family's consternation seemingly disappeared. The famous Leicester detective, nicknamed Tanky Smith because of his stove-pipe hat, went to Spain to try to find him. (Tanky Smith was also a master of disguise and his house on the London Road, known as Top Hat Terrace, has a row of figureheads depicting him in different disguises.) Sadly, although he succeeded in finding him, Joseph Noble had died in a cholera epidemic. This also was the final chapter in the life of Danet's Hall. It was sold to the Leicester Freehold Land Society for building purposes and this was the beginning of suburban expansion in the area. By 1863 the site of the hall and grounds had already been built over. A number of roads off the Hinckley Road were named after major historical figures, including Norfolk Street, on the corner of which the police station stood for many years. The old building still survives but the original 'blue lamp' now hangs outside the new station just across the road.

Hinckley Road, c.1900. The house on the corner, now a lighting shop, had elaborate iron railings.

The mansion house of Westcotes also had a very long history. Originally it had been one of the granges that belonged to Leicester Abbey, with the farmland at Westcotes supplying the Abbey with wheat and other produce. In 1536 it was leased by the abbot and convent to John Ruding, in whose family, with only a brief interval, it was to remain for approximately 300 years. In around 1730 the main façade of the house was rebuilt in brick and designed in the new and fashionable classical style of the period. In 1810, when Walter Ruding was in residence at Westcotes Hall, he became one of the proprietors of the newly reformed *Leicester Chronicle*, continuing its Whig, or Liberal, traditions. Interestingly the same Walter Ruding wrote to Colonel Winstanley on New Year's Day 1824, with an apology 'for interfering in some unspecified business'. Westcotes Hall then

Wyggeston Girls' School playing field in the grounds of Wyggeston hospital, 1913.

King Richards Road, c.1900.

became the property of Thomas Freer, Clerk of the Peace for the county of Leicester. His son, Major Freer, sold it to Joseph Harris, who, along with at least three of his sons, was a solicitor. In 1886 the house and land were sold for building purposes. The first Westcotes Grange was roughly on the site of Cranmer Street today but well back from the Hinckley Road and with the grounds stretching down to Fosse Road.

The present Westcotes House or grange, just down the road and now occupied by the National Health Service Trust, was built for Samuel Harris, one of Joseph Harris's sons. He commissioned a major London architect to design his new house, Samuel Sanders Teulon of Westminster. Teulon had already worked in Leicester in the 1870s when he remodelled Holy Trinity Church on Regent Road. The heavy Gothic and rather dour house was built in around 1886. The 1881 census records Samuel Harris and his five young daughters residing in Westcotes House, with their eight servants.

Dane Hills toll bar, c.1880.

Another solicitor's son, Frederick William Harris, would seem to be the person who had Sykefield built at around the same time, and he lived there until his death in 1950. The Revd Joseph Harris, with money from the sale of the old Westcotes Grange, had the Church of the Martyrs built in 1890, the same year that it became a separate parish. The church, set in a small leafy garden, has some notable commemorative stained glass. Ewan Christian, another architect of national importance, who had designed St Mark's Church some 20 years earlier, was chosen to design the Martyrs. Everard and Pick designed the magnificent Arts and Crafts vicarage, with some Art Nouveau features, in Westcotes Drive, next to the church, in 1904. By this time the area was largely complete, and several streets in the vicinity of the Martyrs Church were named after well-known Protestants, including Livingston, Cranmer and Latimer.

Danet's Hall and Watt's Causeway, c.1860.

The Harris family were generous benefactors and built the delightful little Westcotes School on the corner of Ruding Road and Narborough Road in 1862–3 at a cost of £1,136, designed by major Leicester architects Henry and Joseph Goddard. The building has had a number of uses and was occupied for some years by a branch of Leavesley's hardware stores and then the Elim Pentecostal Church. Shaftesbury Road Board School in Latimer Street was built in 1886 and is still very much in use today as Shaftesbury Junior School. Westcotes Secondary Board School for boys and girls was built in 1903 on the corner of Narborough and Upperton Road. This is another fine, lofty, red-brick building, now Leicester College. At the turn of the century the Westcotes area had a number of small independent schools, usually kindergarten and junior schools, with the senior schools being exclusively for girls. This was no doubt a reflection of the number of middle-class families in the area, gradually increasing from the 1900s with the formation of the new and exclusive suburb of Western Park. The boys would in many cases have been parcelled off to boarding schools while their sisters were educated locally. Miss Ada Ward ran a girls' school from No.193 Hinckley Road. The three-storey semi-detached late 19th-century house opposite Dulverton Road is still there as a private dwelling. The Misses Andrews presided over the Froebel Kindergarten School in Westfield Road as well as at No.72, Fosse Road South. Meanwhile the three Miss Neales operated a school from No.58, Fosse Road Central, which was also their home and that of their father, Thomas Neale, a builders' merchant. Confusingly in the late 1920s two of the Miss Neales, Ethel and Eveline, moved their school, Fosse High School, to

Westcotes Gardens in the snow in the 1960s.

Winter 1876 at the junction of Fosse Road and Westcotes Drive, before the area became built up.

A vehicle accident at the junction of Fosse Road South and Upperton Road in the late 1940s.

No.72. The school continued to operate as a private girls' school from this beautifully designed red-brick, Queen Anne Revival building until it closed in around 1990.

In 1868 a new Wyggeston Hospital designed by T.C. Sorby was built in the area, replacing William Wyggeston's original early 16th-century building near the cathedral.

The same incident, with a policeman taking notes.

For some years Wyggeston Girls' School had its playing fields adjacent to the hospital. This building was demolished in 1966 and a new building designed by Gordon, White and Hood was erected in the grounds. They also planned a commercial site of houses, flats, a public house, petrol station and shops. A pleasant low-rise block of flats now occupies the site of the garage. Many more new streets were laid out towards the end of the 19th century and much of the area to the east was built up by 1900. In the next 40 years the area was to become completely built up. Westcotes has a wonderful mix of housing with eclectic architectural styles, especially in the grand houses on Westcotes Drive and Braunstone Avenue. John Russell Frears had a lofty red-brick house on the corner of Sykefield Avenue and Westcotes Drive designed by Charles Kempson in 1902, in a style which resembled the work of the Scottish architect Charles Rennie Mackintosh. The artisan's dwellings on many of the roads in the area show imaginative designs with some exquisite stained and leaded windows, now sadly disappearing in the name of practicality. The infinite variety of dwellings, with several large houses still in their own grounds, the generous planting of cherry trees and the pleasant Westcotes Gardens all add to the charm of the area, only minutes from the bustle of main roads. In an interview in the *Leicester Mercury* on 17 August 1965, the Misses Read, of nearby Harrow Road, recalled visiting the gardens almost since they were first opened in 1905, on land bequeathed to the city from the Westcotes Estate. They remembered that the men 'were always boater hatted in summer'. There was a bowls club in Sykefield Avenue, where the changing rooms were old cowsheds until at least the 1960s, a legacy of Westcotes Farm.

Fosse Road railway bridge, 1928.

The site of Newarke Girls' School, Imperial Avenue, January 1930.

During the Edwardian period (1901–1910), some very interesting houses were constructed on the corner of Sykefield Avenue and Upperton Road, built by Pick Everard in 1906 and Stockdale Harrison in 1910. In Westcotes too, on Dunster Street and Minehead Street, are to be found a few pairs of Arthur Wakerley's £299 houses built in the 1920s. Dulverton Road was not only home to the Leicester Private Fire Brigade, presided over by Sir Samuel Faire, JP, but also to an aunt of the writer D.H. Lawrence.

As with many areas in suburban Leicester Westcotes was not without its share of allotments, which became invaluable in both World Wars. During World War One the 10 members of the Dulverton Road War Land Association cultivated the site in Westcotes Drive, while the 5th Leicester Scouts made their contribution by growing vegetables on a smaller site nearby. The Hinckley and Narborough Roads are still busy shopping areas, as they were from the late 19th century, but unfortunately in the early 21st century bars are rapidly encroaching on the butchers and bakers.

Further reading:

Beazley, B., *Four Years Remembered: Leicester During the Great War*, The Breedon Books Publishing Company Limited, 1999.

Plant, B., *A Brief History of the Church of the Martyrs 1890–1990*, published by the author, 1990.

Wyggeston Hospital, built in 1870.

Danet's Hall, the home of Dr Noble, c.1862.

Danet's Hall. Dr Noble with his gardener in the 1860s.

Fosse Road Bridge.

WESTERN PARK

The area that was to become the small suburb of Western Park, together with the park of the same name, comprised two areas, the New Parks and Dane Hills. They were barely populated until the 20th century, although the area had seen a great deal of activity when Leicester was occupied by the Romans. There had been a settlement from the 1st century AD until the 4th or 5th century. It is thought that the Romans settled there to quarry the sandstone for the large amount of building work that was taking place in Leicester and the suburb of Westcotes. More than 1,000 years were to pass before the land came into use again; initially as a hunting reserve and from the early 1600s as grazing land for sheep.

The junction of Hinckley Road, Wyngate Drive and Gimson Road, probably taken in the early 1950s.

Local legend has it that a witch by the name of Black Anna or Black Annis lived alone in a cave in the Dane Hills. A withered oak apparently hid the entrance to her bower. History gives her a variety of names and suggests that she was anything from a former Celtic god to a Benedictine Anchoress, in other words a hermit. There are gruesome tales of her pouncing on children who stayed out late in the fields, then sucking the blood from their bodies and hanging their skins up to dry! This rather gory tale still continued to frighten children in the late 19th century, when her cave was apparently destroyed. A major human disturbance occurred in the area in 1485, when Richard III and his army

Western Park, between 1910 and 1914. Little girls are approaching the superb wooden gates, and the new houses on Western Park Road are just visible through the trees.

Old cottages and stables at the corner of Gimson and Glenfield Road, 1972.

marched along the track that is now Glenfield Road on their way to Bosworth Field. Black Anna was said to be the witch that appeared before the King when he struck his foot on a parapet of the old Bow Bridge as he crossed the River Soar. She warned him that his head would strike the same stone on his return to Leicester. Black Anna's prophecy was to come true: the king was killed at the Battle of Bosworth, his body was slung over a horse to carry it back to Leicester and when crossing the bridge his head was said to have

Children playing at Christ the King Roman Catholic Infant and Junior School in 1952, a year after it had opened. On the left is the extremely tall chimney of the Leicester Co-operative Society Dairy. The Victorian building to the right which became part of the school was the former home of Albert Starkey Gimson.

struck the same stone. The Dane Hills were also the scene of a rather unpleasant Easter Monday fair and ritual. The mayor and his councillors, in their official regalia, rode from the mayor's house, it is said, to Anna's Bower Close, somewhere in the vicinity of the present convent of St Catherine. Once there, numerous festivities took place, followed by a hare hunt. In later years a dead cat dipped in aniseed was substituted for the hare, tied to a horse's tail and ridden back to the town, culminating in an excuse for a substantial feast. This annual event survived until the late 18th century. The fair continued until the mid 19th-century. The legend of Black Anna inspired a number of writers including the local poet, John Heyrick (1762– 1797), who penned this gory verse:

Tis said the soul of mortal man recoiled
To view Black Annis's eye, so fierce and wild;
Vast talons, foul with human flesh, there grew
In place of hands, and features livid blue
Glared in her visage; whilst her obscene waist
Warm skins of human victims embraced.

Despite the myths of Black Anna, at the end of the 19th century the area was still relatively rural and peaceful. This was perhaps what prompted the Dominican Order of nuns to build the convent and hospital of St Catherine on the Glenfield Road. A farm and orchard were also part of the complex, and the orchard was still there in the 1990s. The hospital was known for some years as the Home for Incurables and is now St Catherine's Home for Invalids. The convent, built in 1906, was designed by a major Leicester architect, Stockdale Harrison. His son Shirley was to design the De Montfort Hall in 1913 and the Usher Hall in Edinburgh. Next to the convent was New Park Farm, which despite its tranquil setting had problems with the odd poacher. The *Leicester Mercury and Leicester Chronicle* of 22 May 1897 reports that Alfred Henry Mason of New Park Farm; 'was assaulted, as was his bailiff John Howkins, by two men out rabbiting with ferrets.'

The suburb of Western Park, with Letchworth Road at its centre, enjoys a unique position in its proximity to the park of the same name. The area that was to become known as Western Park began to be developed during the 1900s when England, and its empire under King Edward VII, was still a wealthy and powerful nation. Two large country estates previously occupied the area, those of Sir John Mellor, a judge and JP, and William Gimson. After Gimson's death his son, Albert Starkey Gimson, architect and engineer, took over the property. Sir John Mellor's estate was the first to be sold after his death in the 1890s. In 1897 the Town Council purchased 170 acres of land at the very favourable rate of £28,500 for use as a public park.

There was no grand house at the hub of the estate, since John Mellor lived in the south-east of England. There was merely a rather charming early 19th-century farmhouse, with a more severe extension to the rear. The farmhouse, which became the

Sheep grazing on Western Park, c.1904.

park pavilion, is probably best remembered by early local residents as Headley's Tea Rooms, run by Mrs Polly Headley, a baker. The buildings still survive, together with a splendid bandstand, still in use 100 years later. An attractive lodge had been built on the Hinckley Road for the farm, probably in the first half of the 19th century. The park keeper lived at 459, Hinckley Road. Western Park Farm and dairy, run by Mr J.H. Cooper, was just inside the city boundary, further along the Hinckley Road. In the 1920s Mr Cooper had some new stalls erected for his 16 cows with special water bowls, the cows being supplied with warm water in the winter! Albert Gimson, however, in neighbouring Dane Hills, occupied the solid but comfortable mid-19th-century dwelling known as Ashleigh House, on Glenfield Road. Part of the Gimson Estate was an arboretum, where local children occasionally dared to stray, only to be soundly reprimanded if caught by Mr Gimson. In 1951 the house was incorporated into the new building of Christ the King Roman Catholic Primary School. Two other members of the Gimson family commissioned architect Charles Baker in 1884 to design a pair of solid, imposing semi-detached villas on the Glenfield Road, opposite the grounds of Ashleigh House. They were built of local red brick in the fashionable Queen Anne Revival style, incorporating terracotta sunflowers in the brickwork, a particular feature of this style. Revival is perhaps an unfortunate term, as by 1914 the houses were being used as a home for inebriates! They are now halls of residence for De Montfort University students. In early spring 1895 Leicester suffered what the *Leicester Advertiser* of 30 March 1895 describes as a 'hurricane'; three people were killed during the gale and several summerhouses were blown down, as well as damage being caused to allotment gardens on the Hinckley Road.

An electric tram system had been inaugurated for the Western Park area on 12 July

1904. The trams left from the Clock Tower or terminus at Western Park gates at the incredible intervals of every three, three and half, four, four and a half, five and six minutes, taking 14 minutes to reach their destination. The first houses began to appear from about 1905, continuing until the outbreak of World War One. The new suburb was designed in a similar mould to its namesake, Letchworth Garden City in Hertfordshire, but on a much smaller scale. Noted local architects were employed to design the very individual houses, initially on Letchworth Road and Western Park Road. The land forming the boundary with Western Park was a high rocky ridge. This allowed delightful views across the park to the open countryside beyond, but posed an architectural conundrum and a challenge to the landscape gardeners designing the large sites. These problems were solved by having different levels to the front and rear and terracing the gardens as they swept down to the park. Thus the houses fitted perfectly into the landscape. Designs were diverse and many are in the Arts and Crafts style, with a great use of local materials. The housing styles are also a reflection of the involvement of some of the residents in the School of Art, now De Montfort University. Serving on the Art School Committee they came into contact with the most talented local architects and designers of the day. The area was solidly middle-class: there were a number of manufacturers and directors of local companies, with clerks and cashiers in the more modest houses. The area was ideal, and would be described today as a 'small exclusive private development, adjacent to the newest and largest park in the city, complete with bowling green. A tram terminus is conveniently positioned near to the park gates'.

Summer on Western Park.

The area was noted for its healthy atmosphere and it was this that helped to sell the houses. Concerns for heath and fitness were prevalent long before the 21st century! At the end of the 1920s there was a perceived need for a school for delicate children, many of whom lived in the closely packed terraced houses of the inner city. The fresh air of Western Park and the fields beyond was the ideal setting for such a school, and the Western Park Open Air School opened its doors to 180 children in 1930. A *Leicester Mercury* report of November that year describes it as 'The Enchanted School', as indeed it must have seemed to many of its pupils. The report went on to say: 'In place of the fairy coach or enchanted carpet of tradition, every day two special tramcars spirit away lucky boys and girls from the heart of the city to this open-air school.'

The area gradually developed over the next 30 years. Just before World War One Dovelands Infant and Junior school was built, its name arising from the nearby Dovelands Field and small River Dove. It was designed by William Cowdell, the original design being of two storeys, with a separate bonnet room! The only school in the area

Western Park, in the 1920s or 30s.

prior to this was a tiny private school on Westfield Road, the Froebel School, designed in 1912 by R.W. Bedingfield and run by the Misses Edith and Jennie Andrews, who also had a school at No.72, Fosse Road South. Froebel was a method of infant school education promoted by Mrs William Evans, who was to be the first woman member of the School Board. She was the daughter of Joseph Dare, who was greatly involved in the health and education of the poor in Leicester. The building served as St Ann's Parish Rooms for some years and is now the Shiloh Pentecostal Fellowship. The Westfield Road Tennis Club added to the sports and social life of the area. The Church of England was catered for in the shape of a tin hut until the superb church of St Ann's was designed by Cowdell and Bryan and built in 1934. The Mormon Church of Jesus Christ of the Latter Day Saints is on the Glenfield Road.

The park itself proved to be a handy training ground for volunteers to the Leicestershire Regiment at the beginning of World War One, and towards the end of the war the grass on the golf course was harvested to feed horses and cattle. A major event took place on the Whit bank holiday Saturday of 3 June 1916 when a Sopwith Snipe aeroplane named *Leicester* was presented to the Imperial Air Fleet on the Western Park. There had been a government initiative to encourage towns and cities across the country to purchase an aeroplane to expand the Air Fleet. The Leicester Chamber of Commerce rapidly raised 2,000 guineas to buy the aeroplane. The *Leicester Mercury*, reporting on the event, noted: 'There was a pronounced lift in the centre of gravity of the population of Leicester in the direction of Western Park on Saturday afternoon.' Despite initial worries about the weather, the day became hot and sunny and the aircraft, with due ceremony and a cheering crowd of 30, 000 people, took off for France.

The area still remained very much part of the countryside over the next three decades. There was a stile at the end of Letchworth Road leading onto the yet-to-be developed Glenfield Road. This was little more than a track through the fields to Glenfield village

Hinckley Road, c.1890.

until the early 1930s, when roads were extended across the Glenfield Road and other roads created. A small amount of individually designed detached houses were built along with many that were semi-detached, all to a high standard, in a variety of designs. Despite the increase in housing the area was still relatively rural, with open fields between Western Park and Glenfield, the nearest village, until after World War Two, when the New Parks Estate was built. The suburb today has not changed too much since its beginnings almost 100 years ago. The population is still a mix of mainly business and professional people. Very few houses have been added since the 1930s, and the vast green swathe of the park, with its many facilities, is still very much in use.

Interestingly there were no shops in Western Park until the 1960s, when allotments bordering Gimson Road and Christ the King School were sold and a number of houses and flats, with a small shopping area, were created. Until the early 1930s the middle-class residents of Western Park had a large number of high-quality shops on the Hinckley Road beyond the crossroads with Fosse Road. Grocers, butchers and bakers were happy to deliver, a van and a boy on a bicycle being the order of the day. In 1921 the Leicester Co-operative Society opened in Mostyn Street in Westcotes, followed in about 1932 by a row of shops just round the corner on Hinckley Road. The shops are still there today and the two that opened first over 70 years ago are still owned by the same families: Heard's the butchers and Tansley's the hairdressers. Heard's had a van in the 1930s and continued to deliver goods in the Western Park area until the 1990s. Harold Heard was an old Wyggestonian, who took a great interest in his old school, being one of the governors there and also at the nearby Wyggeston Hospital. Like many Leicester businessmen he also found time to be a councillor and was Lord Mayor in the early 1960s. Gilbert Tansley opened his hairdressing salon at about the same time in 1932, and it is still run by the same family today.

In the 1920s, when there were still several farms within a mile or two of Western Park, the Leicester Co-operative Society opened a large dairy on the corner of Glenfield and Gimson Road. Indeed in the 1920s and 1930s it was not uncommon for the odd stray cow to be found happily eating its way through the local gardens. The dairy had one of Leicester's tallest chimneys. When it closed in August 1993, the steeplejack and television personality Fred Dibnah demolished the chimney, in front of a large crowd of excited children and nostalgic Western Park residents. The site is now occupied by some pleasant housing.

Further reading:

Beazley, B., *Four Years Remembered: Leicester During the Great War*, The Breedon Books Publishing Company Limited, 1999.

Creese, G., *Leicester Trams*, Irwell Press, 2000.

POSTSCRIPT

Some of the suburbs of Leicester do not have a section devoted to their area. There was no intention to leave them out but in many instances information was difficult to come by, while others are part of or overlap another area. Photographs for some areas were also virtually nonexistent. Several local authority housing areas are barely documented at all and need much further research. East Leicester has the estates of Netherhall, Goodwood and Thurnby Lodge; these were all post-war housing areas built in the 1950s and 1960s. Thurnby Lodge is by far the largest of these, but it also has an equally large area of private housing adjacent to it. Thurnby Lodge takes its name from the nearby village of Thurnby. Nether Hall, just north of Thurnby Lodge, is reputed to be named after the dower house attached to the hall at Scraptoft, just over the boundary in the county borough. The Anglican churches of St Elizabeth in Netherhall and Christ Church in Thurnby Lodge were both designed by the Graham Wright Partnership in the late 1950s.

New houses on the Goodwood Estate, 1952.

The Hamilton Estate, north of Netherhall, was built from the 1970s onwards on land that had long been the deserted village of Hamilton. At the beginning of the 14th century the village had its own chapel but towards the end of that century only four families remained in the village. Towards the end of the 15th century the chapel was no longer in evidence.

Still in north Leicester, to the west of Humberstone the Northfields and Tailby estates were developed in the 1930s. Northfields House Junior School on Gipsy Lane was once home to fruit and potato merchant, Samuel Brown, whose business operated from the old Wholesale Market in Halford Street. North again is Rushey Mead, sometimes known as Rushey Fields, an extension of Belgrave but an area that has expanded greatly in the second half of the 20th century. The area was once dominated by the large AEI factory on the Melton Road, providing much local employment. Interestingly Rushey Mead was one of the first areas in the city to have cycle lanes. These were laid out in the 1930s when this part of the Melton Road became a dual carriageway. Large numbers of people cycled to work and there were other factories in the area, including the Metal Box Company on Loughborough Road. On Melton Road was the sizeable T.G. Hunt's boot and shoe works. Early in the 20th century they had the rather apt telegraphic address of *Stilleto* (1914 spelling), although it was to be almost half a century before the stiletto heel became fashionable. The area was well served with recreation grounds and allotments and still has many green spaces today. The Anglican church of St Theodore, designed by the Graham Wright Partnership, was built in 1980 and cost something in the region of

Roseneath, 11 St James Road, the home of Frank Staynes of G. Staynes and Sons, Leather Merchants, whose business premises were in Silver Street, 1904.

£150,000. The church combines religious and social spaces and has a very contemporary appearance, which is also reflected in the materials, with white Thermolite blocks being used for the exterior.

North Evington is the area between Spinney Hills and Crown Hills, much of which was developed by Arthur Wakerley as Crown Hills and parts of Spinney Hills had been. The name North Evington is often applied to the whole area and indeed roads like Gwendolen Road, St Saviours and Green Lane Road cross from one area to the other. It is this central area where more industrial works are to be found, many of these being designed by Arthur Wakerley.

North of the city is the post-war estate of Stocking Farm, developed in the 1950s and 1960s, just south of Mowmacre Hill, on the other side of Red Hill Way. The Anglican church of St Luke on Halifax Drive was designed by David Boddington and built over a six-year period from 1960.

Other areas once considered suburban are now much closer to the city centre. The Highfields district was a prosperous middle class area in the 19th century but is now an area rich in multi cultural diversity. By the time of World War Two many of the splendid large Victorian dwellings had become lodging houses. Despite the change in its financial fortunes, there are still many superb buildings and parts of Highfields are conservation areas. St Matthew's Estate was formerly part of the Wharf Street area, once known as 'New Leicester'.

Melbourne Hall, 1900.

Melbourne Hall, with vicar inset, c.1900.

No.17 Melbourne Road.

Further reading:

Brandwood, G.K., *The Anglican Churches of Leicester*, Leicestershire Museums, Art Galleries and Record Service, 1984.

Hartley, R.F., *The Medieval Earthworks of Central Leicestershire*, Leicestershire Museums, Arts and Records Service, 1989.

Willbond, B., *A Home of Our Own 70 Years of Council House Memories in Leicester*, Leicester City Council, 1991.

Melbourne Hall in the 1890s, newly built with incomplete houses in the background.

Saxby Street in 1925.

Garendon Street library.

British Thread Mills, East Park Road, c.1920s.

Saxe Coburg House, the former home of Clement Stretton, c.1890.

Leicester Synagogue, on the corner of Highfield Street and Upper Tichbourne Street, 1961.

Highfields Garage in St Peters Road, as petrol finally comes off-ration in January 1950.

The new Nether Hall estate in 1963.

St Matthew's Estate being built in 1958. St Matthew's Church and Schools are to the right along with the old terraced houses, which would all be demolished by the early 1960s.

Bottom, right: Delivering coal to the topmost flats on St Matthew's Estate in 1965.

Bottom, left: Demolition of 'The Poplars' in Rowley Fields in 1965.

Wharf Street and Russell Square, early 1960s, with the half-built flats of St Matthew's Estate in the background.

Flats under construction, early 1960s, St Matthew's Estate.

The old farmhouse in Stocking Farm where Sunday services took place before St Luke's Church was built. An altar and lectern are set up in the corner, near the window, taken in 1952.

The choir of Thurnby Parish Church in the foreground, with the new Thurnby Lodge Estate Church in the course of construction in 1957.

Building the Stocking Farm Estate in 1952. Note the many factory chimneys and the scaffolding pole serving as a handy coat-hanger.

Looking down on Belgrave from a high vantage point at Stocking Farm, c.1920s.

Thurnby Lodge shops, 1982.

Houses in the course of construction on the Thurnby Lodge estate, using Swedish timber.

Bibliography

Beazley, Ben, *Four Years Remembered – Leicester During the Great War*, Breedon Books, 1999.
Bell, David, *Leicestershire Ghosts and Legends*, Countryside Books, 1992.
Bennett, J.D., *Leicestershire Architects 1700–1850*, Friends of Leicester and Leicestershire Museums, second edition, 2001.
—*Writing About Leicester: A Local History Booklet*, 2000.
Brandwood, G.K., *The Anglican Churches of Leicester*, Leicestershire Museums, Art Galleries and Records Service, 1984.
Brandwood, G. and M. Cherry, *Men of Property: The Goddards and Six Generations of Architecture*, Leicestershire Museums, Art Galleries and Records Service, 1990.
Brown, C. and J. Mills, B. Jarrett, *Beaumont Leys and Home Farm*, Living History Unit, Home Farm Neighbourhood Centre, 1997.
Brown, C., *Leicester Voices*, Tempus Publishing, 2002.
Brown, M., *Leicester Trams on Old Picture Postcards, Reflections of a Bygone Age*, 1995.
Carruthers, A., *Ernest Gimson and the Cotswold Group of Craftsmen*, Leicestershire Museums, Art Galleries and Records Service, 1978.
Couchman, E. (Ed.), *Belgrave as I Remember It*, Leicestershire Libraries and Information Service, 1984.
Cox, T., *Past and Present (St Mary Magdalene Knighton)*, published by the author, 1990.
Cumming, E. and W. Kaplan, *The Arts and Crafts Movement*, Thames and Hudson, 1991.
Creese, Geoff, *Leicester Trams*, Irwell Press, 2000.
Curtis, Revd J., *A Topographical History of the County of Leicester*, W. Hextall, 1831.
Dare, M.P., *Ayleston Manor and Church*, Edgar Backus, 1924.
Elliott, M., *Victorian Leicester*, Phillimore, 1979.
Ellis, C., *History in Leicester*, City of Leicester Publicity Department, 1948.
Ellis, I.C., *Records of Nineteenth Century Leicester*, privately published, 1935.
Ellis, M., *Letters and Memorials of Eliza Ellis*, privately published, 1883.
Fielding Johnson, T., *Glimpses of Ancient Leicester*, Clarke and Satchell, second edition, 1906.
Fox, L. and P. Russell, *Leicester Forest*, Edgar Backus, 1948.
Gill, R., *The Book of Leicester*, Barracuda Books, 1985.
Hartley, R.F., *The Medieval Earthworks of Central Leicestershire*, Leicestershire Museums, Art Galleries and Record Service, 1989.
Hinks, John (Ed.), A*spects of Leicester, Discovering Local History*, Wharncliffe Books, 2000.
Hoskins, W.G., *The Heritage of Leicestershire*, City of Leicester Publicity Department, third edition, 1972.
Lee, J., *Who's Buried Where in Leicestershire*, Leicestershire Libraries and Information Service, 1991.
Leicester City Council, *A Short History of Braunstone Park*, undated.
—*A Short History of Evington Park*, undated.
—*Spinney Hill Park Centenary: 1886-1986*, undated.

Leicester Mercury, *Footpath Rambles Up-To-Date*, F. Hewitt and Son Ltd, 1927.

Millward, R., *A History of Leicestershire and Rutland*, Phillimore, 1985.

Nash, D. and D. Reeder (Eds), *Leicester in the Twentieth Century*, Alan Sutton and Leicester City Council, 1993.

The Pageant Committee, *The Pageant of Leicester City and County*, 1932.

Palmer, R., *The Folklore of Leicestershire and Rutland*, Sycamore Press, 1985.

Pevsner, N., revised E. Williamson, *The Buildings of England, Leicestershire and Rutland*, second edition, Penguin Books, 1992.

Phipps, J., *Leicester in Parliament*, Leicester City Council, 1988.

Plant, B., *A Brief History of the Church of the Martyrs 1890–1990*, published by the author, 1990.

Saffron Past and Present Group, *The Story of the Saff*, Leicester City Council, 1998.

Simmons, J., *Leicester Past and Present, Volume One: Ancient Borough*, Eyre Methuen, 1974.

—*Leicester Past and Present, Volume Two: Modern City*, Eyre Methuen, 1974.

Skillington, S.H., *A History of Leicester*, Edgar Backus, 1923.

Thornton, P., *Clarendon Park*, published by the author, 1990.

—*Old Knighton Story*, published by the author, 1989.

—*The Stoneygate Story*, published by the author, 1986.

Throsby, J., *Leicestershire Excursions*, published by the author, 1790.

Tura, E., *A Roman Occupation Site, Castle Hill-Beaumont Leys*, published by the author, 1986.

The Victoria History of the Counties of England, A History of the County of Leicester, Volume III, Hoskins, W.G. and McKinley, R.A. (Eds), Oxford University Press, 1955.

The Victoria History of the Counties of England, A History of the County of Leicester, Volume IV, McKinley, R.A., (Ed), Oxford University Press, 1958.

Waddington, R.G., *Leicester the Making of a Modern City*, Leicester Corporation, undated.

Willbond, Bill, *A Home of Our Own 70 Years of Council House Memories in Leicester*, Leicester City Council, 1991.

Williams, D.R., *Cinema in Leicester 1896–1931*, Heart of Albion Press, 1993.

Wilshere, J., *Leicestershire (including Rutland) Place-Names*, Leicester Research Section of Chamberlain Music and Books, undated.

—*Old Braunstone*, Leicester Research Department of Chamberlain Music and Books, 1983.

Wrights Directory of Leicester 1914, Kelly's Directories Ltd, 1914.

INDEX